Region and State in Latin America's Past

Johns Hopkins Symposia in Comparative History

The Johns Hopkins Symposia in Comparative History are occasional volumes sponsored by the Department of History at the Johns Hopkins University and the Johns Hopkins University Press comprising original essays by leading scholars in the United States and other countries. Each volume considers, from a comparative perspective, an important topic of current historical interest. The present volume is the twenty-first. Its preparation has been assisted by the James S. Schouler Lecture Fund.

Region and State
in Latin America's Past

Magnus Mörner

The Johns Hopkins University Press
Baltimore and London

© 1993 The Johns Hopkins University Press
All rights reserved
Printed in the United States of America on
acid-free paper

The Johns Hopkins University Press
2715 North Charles Street
Baltimore, Maryland 21218-4319
The Johns Hopkins Press Ltd., London

Library of Congress Cataloging-in-Publication Data

Mörner, Magnus.
  Region and state in Latin America's past / Magnus
  Mörner.
      p.   cm. — (Johns Hopkins symposia in comparative
  history)
  Includes bibliographical references and index.
  ISBN 0-8018-4478-9 (hc : alk. paper)
      1. Central-local government relations—Latin America
  —History—Case studies.   2. Regionalism—Latin
  America—History—Case studies.   3. Latin America—
  Politics and government—Case studies.   4. Latin
  America—Social policy—Case studies.
  I. Title.   II. Series.
  JS2061.3.A3M67   1993
  306.2'098—dc20   92-28774

A catalog record for this book is available
from the British Library.

To Henrik and Jannike,
with gratitude and love

Contents

Tables and Illustrations

Tables

Maps

Graphs

Figures

Preface

DURING THE LAST DECADES, the state, as an independent actor, has emerged from the shadows of social theory where both orthodox Marxism and bland consensus functionalism had placed it. Also, when colonialism had practically vanished in Africa and Asia, not just in Latin America, the need to analyze what the transition from colonial to national rule really meant imposed itself in Eastern Europe, where an almighty state, with its *nomenklatura,* did everything to crush civil society—which has rebounded rapidly since 1989, and hopefully will expand.

The present study focuses on the relationship, over time, between the state in Latin America and civil society on the regional level, which is usually the most durable and dynamic unity in that part of the world. First, I discuss the crucial but controversial concepts of state and region. Then I summarize the major historical changes from the early colonial to the present national state. An overview of the historiography of state and civil society in Latin America follows in Chapter 2; readers with no major interest in historiography are advised simply to leave it aside.

The bulk of the book comprises a series of interrelated case studies, purposely spread out in time and in space. One of the most glaring examples of the contrast between the legal theory of the colonial state and social reality has been chosen to illustrate regional varieties during that era. This is the efforts of the state to impose segregation between Indians and non-Indians, mainly to protect the former. The success of that policy in a region under Jesuit control (until 1768) is merely the exception confirming the general failure of a policy contrary to non-Indian civil society.

The choice that Venezuela made from the 1830s to the 1860s reflects the colonial roots of civil society. Nowhere did racial discrimination in Spanish America remain more pronounced than in Simón Bolívar's native country. This was so because there, in particular, a

wealthy group of mulattoes in late colonial times threatened the socioracial status quo with its tiny white elite. What happened, then, once
legal equality, irrespective of color, was introduced with Independence? In the quest for a general response, I have chosen to highlight
the issue on a regional level.

While from the 1840s onward, Venezuela sank step by step into
civil wars and chaos, the contrary was true in the Brazilian empire from
the 1840s until its sudden fall in 1889. This is why I found it natural
to focus on one of the ambitions of the seemingly strong and stable,
centralized imperial state once the earlier regional attempts to obtain
autonomy in the 1840s had been crushed. No state effort had a more
modernizing character than the introduction of the metric system in
that primitive region in the early 1870s. It is then easier to understand
the popular reaction in the mixed northeastern region.

Finally, the state's promotion of European mass immigration in Argentina, where these ambitions were in many ways extraordinarily successful, has a natural place in these studies. How did native Argentines
react to this increasingly profound transformation of their society? In
other words, what can we find out about the impact of mass immigration on politics? Because free elections were permitted only between
1912 and 1930, logically this is the period on which we have to focus.
For all its political problems, since the 1850s, Argentina had a federal
constitution, in contrast to imperial Brazil. This makes the study of the
political reactions on a provincial level to mass immigration especially
revealing. The answers I have found, as we shall see, are of a rather
paradoxical nature.

Acknowledgments

I HAD THE HONOR of being invited to deliver the James S. Schouler lectures at the Johns Hopkins University in the fall of 1990 by the chairman of the Department of History, Professor A. J. R. Russell-Wood. But the topic was not decided upon all at once. Together the two of us worked on it in the course of rather lengthy correspondence. I soon became fascinated with the idea of linking state policy in Latin America over time with society and power at the regional level. Actually, the present book is the result of more research than might have been expected for a total of four lectures.

At the same time, it must be noted that the book was written in Sweden, far from access to relevant archives. I have become increasingly aware of the severity of this handicap. Regional bibliography, indeed, suffers from many gaps. However, I hope that other historians will use this approach to examine the relationship of the state and civil society on the regional level and that they will use it in more depth than I have been able to do.

I owe a great debt to a number of libraries and their helpful staff members. In geographical order, counted from my desk, they are the Göteborg University Library and the Ibero-American Institute at the same university; the Library of the Stockholm Institute of Latin American Studies and that of the Statistical Central Office, also in Stockholm; the great library of the Ibero-Amerikanisches Institut of Berlin, where I worked intensively for a week in the winter of 1989 and from which I borrowed many materials; and, finally, to fill a last essential gap, the University Library at Cambridge, visited in connection with fulfilling another obligation in that charming city. In connection with my bibliographical problems, I am also grateful to my Berlin friend Matthias Röhrig Assunção for having kindly resolved one of them.

When I lectured in Baltimore in late September 1990, the discussions were very stimulating. I am especially grateful for the constructive remarks by my colleagues Russell-Wood, Franklin Knight, Philip

Acknowledgments

Curtin, and Sidney Mintz. I am also very much obliged to my Swedish friend Roland Anrup for his incisive critical remarks. In the fall semester of 1991, I discussed the manuscript with a small seminar group at the University of Eichstätt, Germany, and I am grateful for their constructive criticism. I cordially thank the anonymous reader employed by the Johns Hopkins University Press for his or her valuable critical suggestions; I thank Ann Waters, the Press's thorough and observant copyeditor; and I thank Phillip King for his skillful indexing. My wife, as always, has been a keen yet encouraging first "judge." Our son Henrik Mörner has been most helpful in preparing several tables, graphs, and correlations with a skill that I do not myself possess.

Region and State *in Latin America's Past*

CHAPTER 1

Introduction: State and Region

The Concept of the State

MORE OFTEN THAN NOT, historians who write about the state as opposed to, let us say, society or the church, do not try to explain what they really mean by the concept. They just take it for granted, whether they belong to a liberal or a Marxist tradition. Still, a closer look at the idea of the state will likely yield a view similar to that of a recent, perspicacious student who offered that it "undeniably is a messy concept" (Mann 1984, 187). The state can be defined in terms of what it looks like, that is, institutionally, or in terms of what it does, that is, functionally.

In 1776, Adam Smith had already combined functions and institutions when making clear that the "sovereign"—that is, the state—had three main duties: first, "protecting the society from . . . violence and invasion . . . by means of a military force" (1887, 2:208); second, "protecting . . . every member of the society from the injustice or oppression of every other member of it [through] an exact administration of justice" (2:227); and third, "erecting and maintaining those public institutions and . . . works, which, though . . . in the highest degree advantageous to a great society, are . . . of such a nature, that the profit could never repay the expense to any individual or small number of individuals." Therefore, because individuals could not be expected to carry out the task, the state had to step in (2:241). Clearly more sensible than some prophets of neoliberalism today, the main founder of liberalism had popular education and communications in mind. In turn, these expenses made state taxation unavoidable (2:241–341).

For Max Weber and his more recent followers, the state is a differentiated set of institutions and personnel that exercise a monopoly of authoritative, binding rule-making, backed up by a monopoly of legitimate use of force. And last but not least, as Weber put it, the state is "a compulsory organization with a territorial basis" (Weber 1978, 1:56; see also Mann 1984, 188).

The younger Marx, especially in "The Eighteenth Brumaire of

Louis Bonaparte," as David Held (States 1983, 27) underscores, found the state apparatus to be simultaneously a "parasitic body" on civil society and an autonomous source of political action.[1] Yet his final and dominant view of the state and its bureaucracy was that they were mere instruments used by the ruling class. This latter view, reinforced by Lenin, gave the Marxist theory of the state a difficult start. In the words of a Soviet textbook from the 1970s, the capitalist state is a "committee running the affairs of the class dominating the economy, an organization which helps it to maintain and consolidate its domination and to rule the whole of society" (Kelle and Kovalson 1973, 181f.). Moreover, from a Marxist perspective, "the state is part of the fabric of society, rather than something apart from, and independent of society," as succinctly put by an English sociologist (Roberts 1981, 23). As is well known, Marx envisioned the demise of the state once the socialist stage had been attained. Contemporary states, which until recently called themselves "socialist," have, indeed, proved him to be deadly wrong on that score. In recent decades, however, many Western Marxists found themselves obliged to grapple with the problem of the state, as it has become increasingly clear in empirical terms that the state does not let itself be reduced to a mere tool of the dominant class. Along somewhat different paths, scholars like Nicos Poulantzas (1973), Perry Anderson (1979), and Göran Therborn (1980) all came to recognize "the relative autonomy of the State." In the view of Therborn, however, "the State should be regarded neither as a specific institution, nor as an instrument, but as a relation—a materialized concentration of the class relations of a given society" (Therborn 1980, 76; also quoted by Skocpol 1979, 28). Christopher Pierson (1984, 567) tries to summarize "postmarxist" theses on the state, two of which, at least, deserve to be mentioned here: (1) "the State does not (either instrumentally or relatively autonomously) function unambiguously in the interests of a single class"; and (2) "the State is not a centralized-unified political actor. It is 'an arena of struggle,' constituted-divided by quite opposing interests."

As historical sociologist Theda Skocpol underlines, both Marxists and their liberal opponents now regard the state precisely as an "arena in which conflicts over basic social and economic interests are fought out" (1979, 25). They just differ with respect to the means used by the state: coercive domination in the view of Marxists, consensually based legitimate authority, according to their liberal opponents. On her part, Skocpol finds that the state is "fundamentally Janus-faced, with an intrinsically dual anchorage in class divided socioeconomic structures *and* [my emphasis] an international system of states." In her view the state is more autonomous than Marxists are able to concede, while the "legitimacy" of the state plays a lesser role than students of the consensus persuasion are willing to admit. Skocpol's view does not lack appeal. Still, I think Michael Mann's ongoing theoretical sociological work will prove more useful as guidelines for the analysis of state activities over time (1984, 1986).

With a Weberian point of departure, Mann makes a basic distinction between *despotic* or direct, forceful power of the state and the state elite, and *infrastructural power,* that is, a capacity to actually penetrate society by imposing its decisions. As such, infrastructural power is compatible with democratic as well as totalitarian regimes. But states may also be "despotically weak," while "infrastructually strong," as contemporary Western democracies are. Feudal states (in the strict, non-Marxist sense) were clearly weak in both respects, while modern authoritarian states tend to exert a high degree of despotic power and are infrastructurally more or less strong as well.

Although the need for state power and its variety of functions have often been discussed, Mann emphasizes the fact of the state exercising power outward from a center but stopping at defined territorial boundaries. Other economic, ideological, and military groupings do not possess such comprehensive, territorially organized power, he claims. This makes the state a socio-spatial organization of its own, an actor embodied in a state elite. It imposes either despotic or infrastructural power or both over groups in society, including regional elites. Mann agrees with, for instance, Poulantzas that the state can be seen as an "arena," a condensation of social relations within its territory, but at the same time, he maintains, it plays a genuinely active role.

Transformations of the State in Latin America

In the case of both Andean America and Meso-America before the coming of the Iberians, state power can certainly be discerned. The discontinuities are such, however, that it is hardly worthwhile to go back so far in this connection. From a later perspective, the formation and fall of the colonial state is what really matters. Portugal and Castile were European pioneers in the formation of early modern European nation-states.[2] From the Catholic kings onward, there was also an ongoing process of coordination of the Spanish kingdoms. As Claudio Veliz (1980) underscores, however, Spanish America from the very beginning was appended to the Kingdom of Castile and owes its centralist tradition to it. Portugal and Castile were also the European pioneers in establishing colonial empires overseas. It is important to notice how, at the same

time, these states used private initiative to make possible such an enormously ambitious enterprise and retained the ultimate power of the
monarchy overseas to make at least some attempt at limiting the rough
display of violence in the course of the Conquest. Thus, the very far-
reaching powers delegated to Columbus and other privileged leaders
"in order that an empire might be founded" (Gibson 1966, 90; in detail,
Pietschmann 1980b) would soon be revoked. Also, later on, local pow-
erholders such as the *encomenderos* of Spanish America and the *dona-
tários* of Brazil would be tamed.

Trade and transportation to the possessions overseas had been su-
pervised by the state from the beginning. A supreme agency for overseas affairs, Consejo de Indias, was established in Spain in 1524; the
Portuguese equivalent came eighty years later. Supreme high courts,
also endowed with administrative powers, *audiencias,* were established
in Spanish America from 1511 onward, and viceroys were sent out to
the *reinos* of New Spain and Peru in 1535 and 1544, respectively. The
monarchs in both Madrid and Lisbon also soon acquired a considerably
stronger control over the church than in their respective European domains. This was so by virtue of the Royal Patronage (Real Patronato of
1508, Padroado real of 1551), the papal concession granted to com-
pensate the respective states for missionary obligation imposed on
them.

The Spanish state in America, and to a lesser extent its Portuguese
counterpart, gradually acquired for its time a relatively high degree of
what Mann terms infrastructural power. Speaking in Weberian terms,
historian John Leddy Phelan thought the Spanish empire was "profoundly patrimonial" but was also, in a somewhat contradictory way,
provided with "pronounced characteristics of feudal, charismatic, and
legal domination" (1967, 326). One of its striking characteristics was
"legal-rational domination," which in Weber's view did not prevail in
the West until the nineteenth century. Phelan rightly pinpointed some
features characterizing Spanish colonial administration that do corre-
spond to that Weberian category (1967, 328–30; see also Pietschmann
1980b, 181f.). For Claudio Veliz, who identified centralism as the main
political tradition in Latin American history ever since colonial times,
the centralist-bureaucratic tradition, in Spanish America at least, satisfied, beyond any doubt, the "key Weberian condition" for legal-
rational domination (Veliz 1980, 7).

The capacity of the colonial state to impose its legal norms and
decisions, however, should by no means be exaggerated. As historian
Horst Pietschmann has also made clear, corruption undermined state

power, everywhere and all the time. Moreover, such widespread corruption constituted a permanent "crisis of conscience" (1982, 29).

As Pietschmann has also suggested, from the theoretical point of view the "colonial state" implies a tricky problem of unity and diversity.[3] We need to start with some legal clarification, however. The overseas kingdoms belonged to the monarch of Castile. The monarch set up special agencies in Castile itself to help him rule these faraway possessions. Special legislation was enacted for their administration. Prior to the Recopilación, or codification of Indian Law in 1681, however, such laws were not necessarily binding for more than one kingdom. The viceroys were sent out—whether to Mexico or Lima—as the king's personal representatives.

Thus, we have to make two sets of distinctions. The king in Madrid ruled two sets of kingdoms—*estos*, Castile, Aragon, and temporarily Sicily, and *esos Reinos*, those overseas—that is, an imperial state in the form of an absolute monarchy. But *esos Reinos* were only linked to him as King of Castile. Due to their subordinate functions within the imperial framework and because of the specifically lower status of their aboriginal and mixed populations, these kingdoms can justly be classified as colonies. Notwithstanding all their legal, economic, and social differences and their usually clear-cut administrative borders, together with the metropolitan agencies for overseas affairs, they formed a single colonial state or empire, just as the Asian, African, and American possessions of the Portuguese king did (see, e.g., Benedict 1974, 552).

Consequently, the breaking up of the Spanish state in 1808 (after all, central administration had been imposed in Spain in 1714) by Napoleon's removal of the legitimate monarch meant that new national states would take shape overseas to replace him and Spain. The Portuguese monarch, on the other hand, had fled to Brazil, which helped to make Brazil's transition easier and to maintain its territorial integrity. The new states of Spanish America were based on colonial administrative patterns (more often than not on the *audiencia* level). As Pietschmann also observes, however, this pattern of organization does not justify the automatic assumption of previously existing protonational colonial states and societies. I believe rather that we have to consider parts and variations of a common, though far-flung "colonial state" and a number of regional societies.

Certainly, the colonial state, during three centuries of domination, occasionally had to resort to armed force against rebellions. Yet it was not until the later eighteenth century that colonial authorities had mobile forces at their disposal for that purpose. At the same time, as

Pietschmann (1980a, 169) rightly underlines, the later eighteenth century reform period with its administrative reorganization implied an important step toward the internal state formation in the former colonies. It did create the administrative structure required to establish any national state at all. The predominant feature of colonial Latin America was bureaucratic, peaceful rule, reinforced by means of the Bourbon and Pombaline administrative reforms.[4]

Consequently, the contrast with the violent, postcolonial, early national period could hardly be more striking. The dependence of the *caudillos* (or strongmen on regional or national levels, who seize power with extralegal means) on despotic power had a counterpart in their utterly weak infrastructural power. The legitimacy of the new states and their rulers was also very weak. Instead of forming parts of an essentially unified empire, as they had done so far, the newborn Spanish American states, paradoxically from a European perspective, had to help in creating their own nations, rather than the other way around.[5]

During the latter part of the nineteenth century, the state in most of the Latin American countries was able to attain a rather high degree of consolidation and once again an increase in infrastructural power. Historian Marcello Carmagnani (1984), by terming the period of 1880–1914 in Latin American history that of the "Oligarchical State," makes clear his view that the oligarchy determined the character of the state during this lapse. With a Weberian definition of the state as his point of departure, for instance, historian Lorenzo Meyer (1974) denies that there was a state in Mexico prior to the era of Porfirio Díaz, that is, from the 1870s until 1910. However, with the 1910 Revolution, the state "vanished" until it was reconstructed under President Carranza ten years later (722, 726).

In general terms, the period 1914–30 witnessed the integration of new social strata with political life, such as urban middle- and working-class groups, and the state was invigorated thanks to external influences as well as Latin American reformist or revolutionary efforts. From the perspective of the present time, the advanced stage of crisis in which Latin America finds itself today can be traced back rather easily to the profound changes—economically, politically, and socially—that set in with the Depression. This development has certainly meant, as sociologist Marcos Kaplan puts it, "growing state autonomy and intervention, authoritarianism and neo-fascism" (1986, 277). It has not carried with it the disappearance of despotic power (at times, on the contrary, it has been roughly displayed), but merely a slow growth in infrastructural power. The latter, at least, has remained most unevenly distributed over the various national territories.[6]

State and Region

When discussing the reactions to state decisions, I opt for doing it on a regional level. The term *region,* however, is used in a vague and ambivalent way more often than not. Also, regions are not static over time but are normally modified under the impact of economic, demographic, logistical, and administrative changes. For geographer David J. Robinson (1979), who studied spatial patterns of colonial Latin America, the "regional" or *meso* level normally pertains to a city or large town with its hinterland.[7] For him, the *macro* level is "historic super-regional," that is, a viceroyalty or one or two *audiencias;* these are generally the areas that became national states after Independence. The local or *micro* level, on the other hand, naturally corresponds to a parish/municipality or perhaps an urban *barrio.*

Super-regional and regional diversity and the often great distances between regional centers very soon caused Spanish colonial centralism to be considerably modified. On the super-regional level, this was clearly recognized by the delegation of royal power to viceroys and *audiencias,* far more extensively in administrative practice than according to legal norms, however. The administrative centers, on that level, housed the high bureaucracy and the leading merchants. Later, in their capacity as national capitals, they would continue to do so and usually to an even greater extent during the national period.

However, in many respects, regions (i.e., the meso level) are more rewarding for historical analysis. They are more homogeneous in geographic and at times ethnic terms. At this level, the formation, concentration, and distribution of wealth can be studied in relation to changing market conditions. Thus, we can also observe, at close quarters, the formation and changing composition of regional elites. Their strength and weakness were normally inverse to those of the elite at the macro or state level. With respect to the Wars of Independence, John Lynch (1984, 203) underlines that the *caudillo* was always a "regional chief," who drew on clients and resources at both regional and local levels. To be sure, some *caudillos* would ultimately seize control at the new national level. Yet their power remained personal, not institutional, as Lynch maintains.

Clearly, the national level is not merely a compilation summing up all the regions but contains psychological, political, and cultural dynamics of its own. National averages in statistical terms, however, sorely need regional data as correctives, as they may often appear fictional in relation to the various, often contrasting, regional realities. Moreover, as anthropologist John Gledhill (1988, 302) reminds us, "differences between regions and their relationship to the class structures which have emerged over the long term within particular Latin American nation-states" are of basic importance. Thus, different "national trajectories in the nineteenth and twentieth centuries reflect the way different regions interact historically within larger configurations." This implies that regional unevenness becomes an important factor that needs to be analyzed in a comparative perspective.[8]

Under these circumstances, the interaction between state and regions becomes a very important theme in Latin American history. Usually, however, it has only been studied in either a colonial or a contemporary context. As I have already stated, my intention is to present a few case studies taken from a broad range of contexts in time and space of social, economic, and political as well as comparative analysis.[9] At times such reactions or lack of reactions to state decisions may merely reflect the attitudes of members of the regional elites. On other occasions, however, they may have a more popular character, as in the case of the so-called Quebra Quilos revolts in northeastern Brazil in the 1870s. Political reactions may take the form of nonparticipation, as with respect to immigrants in Argentina during the early twentieth century.

CHAPTER 2

State and Civil Society in Latin America: A Historiographical Discussion

BROADLY SPEAKING, the concepts of state and civil society cover the entire range of interplay between political and socioeconomic history. As John Tosh (1984) puts it, political history is "the study of all those aspects of the past, which have to do with the formal organization of power in society, which for the majority of human societies in recorded history means the state" (66). With reference to "civil society," until the mid-eighteenth century, according to John Keane (1988, 35), it was "coterminous with the state."

Then a differentiation took place. During the era of the American and French revolutions, the idea even emerged that civil society might be justified in defending itself against the state (Keane 1988, 33). But soon Jeremy Bentham and others would emphasize that civil society often needs strict state regulation and control. Along similar lines, German philosopher G.W.F. Hegel argued in 1821 that civil society formed an intermediate phase between family and state, and that it was a "sphere of social life where individuals pursue their own self-interest within universally recognized bounds" (Mann 1983, 45). Hegel located the moving principle of civil society primarily in the *Bürgerstand* (the bourgeois estate).[1] Karl Marx, in turn, interpreted Hegel's notion of civil society as "material interaction between individuals" during the capitalist stage. At the same time, he made clear that "the State, the political order, is the subordinate, and civil society, the realm of economic relations, is the decisive element." Thus, civil society transcends both state and nation, Marx states, although "it must assert itself in its foreign relations as a nationality, and inwardly organize itself as a state" (Keane 1988, 633f., 81ff.). This is the starting point for the long-time Marxist neglect of the study of the state. Outside Marxism, civil society has generally become understood to be socioeconomic life as distinct from the state.

9

Against this backdrop, most of the historiography on Latin America should be expected to take up one aspect or another of this crucial relationship between state and civil society. Certainly, many of the data which the historians have provided are relevant for such a discussion. Yet most historians by far have not been overly interested in theoretically explicit discussions, and they seldom even bother to define the concepts they use. They do not often analyze the changing relationship between state and civil society over time in more general terms. Therefore the present discussion will be concerned only with those historians who constitute fortunate exceptions to the general lack of interest in theoretical concepts and analysis during the post-1945 era.

In the tradition of Rankean historicism, with its Prussian background, the state always occupied a place of honor. As the late historicist Friedrich Meinecke (1862–1954) put it, the state is "the causally most influential factor of historical life" and will always so remain (Stern 1956, 286). The great Latin Americanist historian Richard Konetzke (1897–1980) was a student of Meinecke's. Thus, his positive view of the role of the state in Spanish America prior to Independence is hardly surprising. His view is expressed most clearly in an article from 1951 (reproduced in 1983, 319–44). Konetzke starts by clarifying that state and society are two "forms of configurations of the collective human experience" that are autonomous and essentially different, at the same time that they are also "subject to continuous change." Moreover, they are mutually dependent. With respect to Spanish America, Konetzke underlines that even though Spaniards brought their social values and institutions with them to the New World, the Spanish state intervened very forcefully in the process of social formation in America, which he then proceeds to analyze, aspect by aspect. In the introduction to his important anthology of royal decrees and so on in Spanish American social affairs, 1493–1810 (1953/62, 1:vii), Konetzke, without any reservations, affirms that "metropolitan legislation was an essential factor in the formation of colonial society."

Without Konetzke's explicit ambition to derive the history of society from that of state legislation, another historian, Chilean Mario Góngora, placed his great work on state formation in Spanish America, 1492–1570, squarely in the context of Spanish American law (*derecho Indiano*). At the same time, Góngora underlined the importance of the nonapplication of the law (1951, 282–85). In a later, shorter version (1975), Góngora most interestingly concludes that, with one minor exception, the institutional characteristics of the state in the Indies were very much the same as those of the state in Spain. And the "one authentically 'American' factor was the impossibility of a thoroughgoing enforcement of the underlying legislative notions and of the Spanish conception of the State, on account of the immense distances involved, ethnic diversity and the tendency in the colonial environment to escape legislative provisions that proved burdensome." Extending his reasoning to the Americas in general, he even affirms that this was a peculiarly American form of liberty "outside the framework of the State, in contrast to the Liberty within the State existing in the European Middle Ages [!]. Liberty in the Americas was not based . . . on any new concept of the State: it was rooted in laxity: it was, in other words, essentially 'colonial'" (126f.). This passage could be criticized both for idealizing medieval European "liberty" and for vaguely linking "laxity" to "colonial."

Góngora's study (1951) was one of the points of departure for my own ambitious attempt (1970) to analyze a particular set of laws (the segregation policy of excluding non-Indians from Indian towns) with regard to their casuistic background and, above all, the crucial procedure of law enforcement attempted by the state, be it through administrative or judicial action. As I saw it, the failure of imposing the segregation policy could initially be explained simply in terms of the weakness of the executive administrative and the judicial apparatuses. In addition, in this case, the segregation policy was also doomed to failure because it was opposed by very strong demographic and social forces in the countryside. In 1988, a specialist in the realm of *derecho Indiano,* Ismael Sánchez Bella, confirmed my sad impression, however, that since 1970 the problem of law application hardly received any further attention at all on the part of the historians in the field, at least as far as the colonial period was concerned (Balance 1989, 445f.).

Max Weber (1864–1920), with his exceptionally keen analytical mind, gave the state all due attention. In precise terms, he defined it as a "compulsory organization with a territorial basis," holding a monopoly on any legitimate use of force, something "as essential to it as its character of compulsory jurisdiction and of continuous operation" (1978, 1:56). Weber's discussions of charismatic and legitimate authority, patrimonial administration, rational-legal bureaucracy, and so forth have influenced generations of social scientists (even if some generations, such as the present one, have been influenced more than others). It was not until the 1960s that some students of Latin America's past took up some of Weber's ideas.

Within his study of the *audiencia* of Quito in the seventeenth century, American historian John Leddy Phelan (1967) discussed Spanish colonial administration in Weberian terms. Certainly, charismatic features were present. Phelan stresses the "central importance of the mystique of the monarchy" (322). With respect to the patrimonial state with its feudal roots, Phelan emphasized the predominance of "the corporate principle that the individual's rights, privileges and obligations were derivative from the particular estate and functional corporations to which the individual belonged." As in late medieval times, the monarch was primarily "the supreme judge," from which role his administrative authority also derived (323f.). Richard Morse already observed that the Weberian typology of the "patrimonial state describes with surprising accuracy the structure and logic of the Spanish Empire in America"(1964, 157f.). Phelan also points at the high degree of flexibility of administration and law as indicators of patrimonialism. At the same time, however, Phelan also discerns important traits of legal domination in the Spanish colonial system, "in a bewildering combination" (329) with patrimonialism. In this respect, Spanish America did in fact foreshadow the predominance of legal-rational domination that according to Weber did not prevail in Europe until the nineteenth century. Phelan does not finish his analysis, however, but refers to sociologist S. N. Eisenstadt (1963), who had added a fourth category, "historical bureaucratic polity," which in my view actually blurs the discussion. Phelan's attempt was a very interesting though inconclusive one which apparently left few traces in the historiography on Spanish America.[2]

During the 1970s, the state–civil society dichotomy almost vanished from the awareness of both social scientists and historians.[3] In the mainly empirical and narrative Anglophone historiographical tradition, "state" continued to be replaced by the term "government," supposedly self-explanatory. As political scientist Alfred Stepan (1978) rightly underlined in a book on the Peruvian state, however, state certainly means more than "government." The state attempts not only "to structure relations between civil society and public authority . . . but also to structure relationships within civil society as well" (xii). The only context in which the state concept continued to be normally employed was the dichotomy of state and church. In Latin America, of course, until the late nineteenth century, at least, their relationship had normally been uneasy. Yet, during the colonial period and as long as the church remained that of the state, this relationship was basically one between two branches of administration. During the 1970s, analytically and theoretically minded historians were above all engaged in the study of social structures, sometimes with the help of quantification and with either functionalist or Marxist perspectives. Orthodox Marxists and others still exclusively concerned with the impact of class on politics continued to let "the state . . . be written off as the political arm of whatever class happens to enjoy 'hegemony.'"[4]

Among West European "neo-Marxists," however, there was a trend in favor of admitting the state "a certain autonomy vis-à-vis the class it primarily represents" (Tosh 1984, 145f.). Antonio Gramsci (1891–1937) already had stressed the importance of the concept of "hegemony," which rested on a rough congruence of values between the political leadership and civil society. Moreover, as Gramsci put it, "between the economic structure and the State with its legislation and its coercion stands civil society" and the "State is the instrument for conforming civil society to the economic structure" (Held et al. 1985, 122). Louis Althusser underlined that the state apparatus plays an active role in shaping the values in civil society, and his disciple Nicos Poulantzas went even further, in 1973, in asserting the relative autonomy of the state. At the same time, Göran Therborn (1980), of the same group, declared, however, that "the State as such has no power: it is an institution where social power is concentrated and exercised" (132). In 1974, Perry Anderson found fit to remind fellow Marxists about the axiom that "secular struggle between classes is ultimately resolved at the political—not the economic or cultural—level of society." In his *Lineages of the Absolute State* (1979 [1974]), Anderson keenly analyzed the varied impact of imperial wealth on the economy and state power of Spain (11, 60–84).

As a student of social revolutions, historical sociologist Theda Skocpol (1979), who studied with Barrington Moore, retorted to the neo-Marxists that we can make some sense of such revolutionary transformations "only if we take the state seriously as a macrostructure." The state "is no mere arena in which socio-economic struggles are fought out" but "a set of administrative, policing and military organizations, headed, and . . . coordinated by an executive authority" (29).

In Latin American studies, the new approaches of neo-Marxists and other social scientists of mixed Weberian and Marxian heritage were, naturally enough, first used in the field of contemporary politics. Latin American and Latin Americanist social scientists tried to explain the compatibility between the increasingly important role of the state in the developmental process and nondemocratic political structures since the 1960s. Two conceptual frameworks came into being: the state capitalist and the bureaucratic-authoritarian perspectives, the latter with Guillermo O'Donnell (1978) as its main representative. Although from the 1960s onward dependency theories tended to reduce the role of national politics and the state, O'Donnell found the new "bureaucratic-authoritarian State in Latin America to be the recent product of the crisis of import substitution, industrialization and of populism" (Mitchell 1988, 72f.; Stepan 1985, 317f.).

The increased interest in the state also spilled over to some Latin American and Latin Americanist historians with receptive minds. As one of them, Pietschmann (1987), has rightly observed: "This rediscovery of the state concept by the historiography on Latin America, however, was not accompanied by a theoretical debate as in social sciences. In turn, from this probably follows the enormous vagueness with which the concept is used in historical bibliography" (430).[5] However, a series of efforts explicitly aimed at highlighting the role of the state and the historical development of societies in Latin America in more modern terms deserves to be discussed briefly.

To begin with, I believe that the special issue on the Mexican state of the journal *Historia Mexicana,* published by El Colegio de México in 1974, can be characterized as a pioneering initiative. It did not present a unified approach, however. Bradley Benedict found the state, from 1519 to 1700, to be a "colonial State, a subdivision of the Imperial State," paradoxically weak and omnipotent at the same time (552, 605). David Brading, on the other hand, preferred to analyze the eighteenth-century state in terms of a bureaucracy-elite relationship. Lorenzo Meyer, finally, supported by the Weberian notion that the state must exercise an efficient monopoly on legitimate violence over a certain territory, even denied that such a state existed at all in Mexico between 1810 and 1870 and, of course, once again, between 1910 and 1920.

Also in 1974, a group of former students of American historian Lewis Hanke published a suggestive and useful methodological anthology of Latin American history (Graham and Smith 1974). In this volume, Margaret E. Crahan, Stuart Schwartz, Frank Safford, Richard Graham, Joseph Love, and Peter Smith all took up issues more or less relevant to the state-society dichotomy. In her study, Crahan stressed that the metropolis, Spain, far from being a new nation-state in 1492 itself, as so often asserted, had not become one even when the colonies made themselves independent. In America, the patrimonialism of the colonial system, moreover, was followed by the creation of a "neo-patrimonial" national state and a quest for state legitimacy.

In 1980, Claudio Veliz, a Chilean-born sociologist at an Australian university, published his innovative book on the *Centralist Tradition of Latin America.* For Veliz, as opposed to Phelan, it was quite clear that centralism belonged to the Weberian category of rational domination and was a most important trend in Latin America for two hundred years prior to the French Revolution. Even though central control was obviously weakened during the periods 1600–1760 and 1850–1930, Veliz maintained that in Latin America *grosso modo* "political tradition . . . has always been centralist" (5, 9). In this connection it is worthwhile to recall that American historian Woodrow Borah, when looking at contemporary Latin American politics in 1963, had already found "a series of survivals which may be grouped under the term centralization. Whatever the legal fiction of local autonomy, the province captures power and revenues from the local units, and the national government in turn strips states and provinces of sustenance and vigor." Borah derived that phenomenon from the reforms of the late eighteenth century (Borah, Gibson, and Potash 1963, 373f.).

Another initiative was taken in 1982 by Italian historians Ruggiero Romano and Marcello Carmagnani when they devoted volume 5 of their journal *Nova Americana* to the historical forms of the state in Latin America. Their point of departure was to reject the prevailing trend to identify state and nation in Latin American contexts. According to Romano and Carmagnani, this impeded an understanding of how the modern state emerged in the various parts of Latin America. From a general and theoretical point of view, the study of the colonial state versus local and regional power by the Colombian historian Hermes Tovar Pinzon and that of Horst Pietschmann on bureaucracy and corruption in colonial Spanish America were especially noteworthy. Pietschmann (1982) clearly goes beyond the more institutional (*verfassungsgeschichtliche*) approach characterizing his earlier works on the colonial state (1980a, 1980b). In his article, with a Marxist frame of reference, Tovar (1982) makes an interesting attempt to separate the metropolitan from the colonial (or viceregal) state in their relationship to the emerging power centers on regional and local levels.

Making use of the Bolívar Bicentenary in 1983, four German historians, former students of Konetzke (Pietschmann among them), organized an international symposium on the formation of state and nationhood in Spanish America (Problemas 1984). Because of the heterogeneous character of the group of historians invited to participate and their freedom to choose their approaches, it is difficult to evaluate the volume. Yet the editors rightly underline that the priority given to the state or the nation formation process depends on the historian's perspective. When the subject matter is seen from today's perspective, early types of national consciousness tied to regionalisms preceded the emergence and territorial delimitations of the state. On the other hand, those students who find social integration to be a basic requirement for the existence of a nation will naturally find that the state preceded the nation and, consequently, the nation-state.

In 1985, Carmagnani and some other Italian Latin Americanist historians organized a meeting in Florence, the proceedings of which also bring together a great number of interesting contributions on

Latin America's transition from a colonial state to a *stato nazione* (Annino 1987). In a fascinating chapter of introduction, Ruggiero Romano (1987) discusses the concepts of nation, state, and freedom in a comparative European and Latin American context. He finds the striking persistence of "oligarchies" in Latin America to be due to the ever-increasing gap between state and civil society. At the same time, he makes clear that in his view the state is essentially an intermediary between power and civil society.[6] Most of the papers included are rather circumscribed in time or space. Once again, that of Pietschmann (1987) deserves more general interest. It deals with the colonial state of the eighteenth century facing the different value systems ("mentalities") of the various socioethnic groups. In his view this problem forced the Bourbon administration to a very selective application of legal norms. In turn, Pietschmann suggests, this may have contributed to the imperial collapse and the weakness of the new states. In his article, Pietschmann also points at a basic problem which remains to be resolved. Should the whole of one colonial power, be it Spain or Portugal, be considered one colonial state which would be succeeded by a number of national states? Or should the existence of previous "proto-national" entities be recognized as the predecessors of each national state? (429f.) In a later study (1989), Pietschmann also poses the question of when the various administrative units of the Empire were actively replaced by so many states (149).

In 1986, two French Andinist scholars, J. P. Deler and Yves Saint-Geours, produced an interesting anthology, *Estados y naciones en los Andes* (States and nations in the Andes), with the participation of Peruvian, Bolivian, Ecuadorean, Colombian, and French scholars. The editors of the two volumes, based on a meeting in Lima in 1984, rightly point out that by 1815, Europe still was (or, rather, had returned to) "l'ancien regime or multinational Empires." In Central and Eastern Europe, the nation-state would not come into being until the 1920s. Thus, in some ways, the Latin American states even played a pioneering role.[7] Republican constitutions and liberalism clearly proclaimed were earlier in Latin America than in Europe. "Therefore, are these countries really Nation-States or simply national States? Are they something more than territorial states?" (Deler and Saint-Geours 1986, 1:21f.)

Firmly organized, the meeting concluded that the study of the formation of national societies would require a clear, empirical distinction between the "ruling group" and the "dominant class." Also, not just the national projects of the elites but also the popular "counter-projects" of the suppressed strata would deserve to be scrutinized (1:349–51). Moreover, participants seem to have agreed that even if "nation-state" is not an appropriate term in the case of the nineteenth-century Andean states, Independence gave rise to territorial states which at times carried out "national tasks" and created new regional patterns (2:666). As summarized by Marie Danielle Demelas at the meeting in Lima, the importance of the confusion between the state and private spheres was also underlined.

During the 1980s, special aspects of the state-society relationship have been explored in a number of important monographs. One aspect is that of the Indians, as actors as well as objects in the colonial system (Mörner 1987). A mighty monograph is *Justice by Insurance* by Woodrow Borah (1983) on the General Indian Court of Mexico during the colonial period. The crucial question of application is hardly taken up, however. More thrilling, perhaps, is the study by the Welsh ethnohistorian Tristan Platt of the relationship between the national state of Bolivia and the Indian *ayllus* (communities) in one part of the country (1982). It shows that, notwithstanding its anti-Indian stance, the state of the *criollos* for a long time failed in its attempts to crush the communities.

At least outside Spain, the relation between state and church, often studied in the past, during recent years has been relatively neglected by historians. The proceedings of a meeting on church, religion, and society in Latin America prior to 1945, held in Hungary in 1987 (Iglesia 1989) provide us with current coverage, however. A bold attempt at new interpretation of the dramatic struggle between state and church in Ecuador, 1780–1880, by two French historians, Demelas and Saint-Geours (1988), should also be noted.

Increasingly, historians and social scientists have become aware of the importance of the chains of vertical patron-client relationships in Latin America over time. *Caudillo* control on local, regional, and national levels, for example, cannot possibly be analyzed outside this broader context. Also, as sociologist Eisenstadt and his collaborator Luis Roniger (1984) put it, from the mid-nineteenth century onward, "the machinery of the new states penetrated peripheral areas, and the development of parliamentary politics, based on a slowly but continually expanding franchise, induced the emergence of political patron-client networks on a wide scale. In peripheral areas, *caciques*, as they were called in Mexico, in Brazil, *coroneis*, bargained over votes they could deliver with political forces at the regional or national levels" (100f.). Thus, the phenomenon is really at the heart of the state–civil society dichotomy.

The most important recent monograph is no doubt that of Richard Graham (1990) on patronage and politics in imperial Brazil. In the author's view, patronage in nineteenth-century Brazil "sustained virtually every political act" (2). The Brazilians in general, he claims, did realize that "an impersonal state remained a pipedream." Instead, they believed that "the provision of employment and the distribution of authority constituted the true and lasting function of the state." The interests of the propertied elite were mainly advanced by the state "by reproducing and maintaining the patron-client system itself." Thus, "patronage provided the major link between Society and State" (272). Moreover, with new actors and partly new forms, patronage would also continue to prevail after 1889, as shown, for example, by Linda Lewin in her monograph (1987) on the related phenomenon of *parentela* (kinship) and politics in Paraíba during the early Republic.

The present trend toward giving the state and its role for society greater attention in historical research seems quite clear. So it is in political science, sociology, and anthropology as well. Consequently, a discussion such as the present one can only serve as a short historiographical introduction as of 1992 to a quickly growing body of research.

CHAPTER 3

The Segregation Policy of the Colonial State

THE POINT OF DEPARTURE for the Spanish social policy in the Americas was the idea of the two "Repúblicas," that of Spaniards and that of Indians. Natural at first, this division soon became undermined by the process of race mixture in which imported African slaves would also take part. Also, at first it appeared natural that secular Christian Spaniards would facilitate the process of christianization by setting the Indian converts a "good example." Even Fray Bartolomé de las Casas, for all his condemnations of Spanish cruelties, thought that at the least carefully selected Spaniards would do so. Soon, however, both he and other missionaries realized that more often than not the opposite was true.

Thus, Las Casas's famous experiment in eastern Guatemala, the so-called Tierra de Vera Paz, was carried out by his Dominican missionaries without any other Spaniards. But this exclusion was a local and temporary privilege granted to these missionaries. A consistent policy of gathering Indians into nuclear settlements of the Mediterranean type, with their own municipalities (*cabildos*) but under missionary guidance (*reducciones*), took form in the latter part of the sixteenth century. Thus, in order to protect the Indians, the state saw fit to gather the Indians and the so-called Spaniards (an increasingly mixed lot), respectively, into similar but separate towns or villages. One category of non-Indians after another was then prohibited from settling down in the Indian towns. In the "Spanish" towns, Indians were supposed to live in particular quarters (*barrios*). This is the segregation policy we are going to study on a regional level.

First, let us establish a basic understanding about the nature of Spanish American legislation. Theoretically, law always derived from the king (in council). There were no clear distinctions between law, administration, and the administration of justice. Most royal dispositions were addressed to a particular authority overseas and were not necessarily valid for others. Such dispositions had been obtained by a party, often a visitor at court, to remedy a particular grievance. Thus, legislation was clearly casuistic and soon became overwhelmingly extensive. It became an almost impossible task for authorities in the Indies to keep all these, often contradictory, legal norms in mind.

Things became easier with the publication of a lawbook, the *Recopilación de Leyes* of 1681, a selection of 6,377 royal dispositions, explicitly valid for *esos Reinos de las Indias*, that is, the colonial empire. Here, the prohibition against non-Indians living among the Indians was clearly stated in no less than ten different laws. The prohibition even included Spaniards who had received *encomiendas*, that is, trusteeships over the Indians of a certain village, and Spaniards who wanted to live there. Merchants and other Spaniards could visit an Indian town for three days but not more. It is possible to study the specific context of each one of these dispositions. Some were issued around 1550, others in 1563 and mainly concerned with Peru. The basic prohibition came in 1578, as the result of intensive lobbying at the Court by a Franciscan friar from Peru (Mörner 1962). It was complemented in 1618 and 1646 (explicitly including those who had acquired land in the jurisdiction of an Indian town).

Segregation harmonized rather well with other state aims, such as using different kinds of clergy for the two republics, and different justices, to "depersonalize" the relation between the *encomenderos* and "their" Indians, to protect Indian agriculture from damage caused by the cattle herds of the "Spaniards," and to keep the Indians apart from the blacks, mulattoes, and mestizos considered especially inferior and pernicious. On the other hand, the segregation policy certainly did not harmonize with the hopes of the state to "hispanize" the Indians.

When it comes to the application of the law, once again we have to emphasize that the borders between administration and justice were blurred, even if viceroys and governors were primarily administrators and the *audiencias* were primarily legal courts. On the level of viceroys, with respect to segregation (and in many other matters as well), we notice that toward 1600 they found fit to interpret the metropolitan commands rather amply. They were really only concerned with those who actually gave the Indians a very "bad example." The vigorous Viceroy of Peru, Francisco de Toledo, declared in 1572 that segregation had been useful during the turbulent period of the past but was no longer so. On the contrary, married mestizos and most *encomenderos* should be encouraged to settle down among the Indians—but blacks should not.

Yet from Madrid, increasingly pathetic commands imposing segregation strictly continued to be sent to viceroys and *audiencias*. Any

The Segregation Policy of the Colonial State

Real Cédula received was supposed to be made public, together with the decision of local authorities imposing deadlines and sanctions for violations, by being read aloud by the "town crier" (*pregonero*) in the main plaza. To be sure, cases can be found in which administrative action was, in fact, taken to carry out the segregation policy in this way. Because the sanction normally just implied that the persons in question be thrown out of the settlements where they lived, however, the result of such action was bound to be ephemeral, at best a merely temporary change. It was only when such expulsions were combined with the founding of new Spanish towns that gathered such non-Indians from the countryside that administrative action had any potential at all. In the course of the seventeenth century, the establishing of such towns ceased. From this time onward, the authorities either granted appeals from those non-Indian settlers who were threatened with expulsion to remain living among the Indians, notwithstanding the segregation laws, or relapsed into passivity on the whole issue.

On the other hand, judicial action would take place occasionally even after the seventeenth century for the obvious reason that the persons accused by the plaintiff (whether the Indians or a priest) were sentenced with expulsion for actually being pernicious. Yet, however often sentences imposing expulsion (usually for life) were passed, and the culprits were notified and accepted that sentence, actual expulsion seldom seems to have taken place. The local Spanish officials on the lowest level (*corregidores de indios*) were too corrupt, too lazy, and often themselves too involved with the culprits to act. Also, the existing administrative control machinery (*jueces de comisión*) was simply too cumbersome and costly to function in such cases. And appeals were filed interminably by the culprits. Thus, in Mann's terms, the state's infrastructural power was certainly weak with respect to this area of legislation, because sufficiently strong social forces on the regional and local levels could not be mobilized to help impose its decisions. Indians were probably mostly, but not always, in favor of residential segregation, and so were at the least many parish priests. On the other side, however, the pressure mounting from the swelling strata of landless mestizos, mulattoes, and other poor non-Indians, who had usually grown up in the Spanish towns, to somehow take over the lands held by an Indian population in decline proved to be decisive. On the whole, from the late sixteenth century onward, segregation was doomed. The following brief sketches of three regional cases, however, illustrate the various kinds of social change, vested interest resistance, and administrative inertia involved in this conspicuous failure of the colonial state.[1]

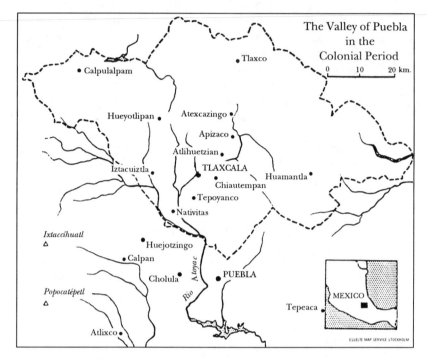

Map 1. Tlaxcala during the Colonial Period.
Source: Mörner 1970, 265

Tlaxcala

To the east of Tenochtitlán, the people of the independent city-state of Tlaxcala had been an invaluable ally of the Spaniards in the course of the overthrow of Aztec domination (1519–21). Whether based on a promise by Cortés or not, the city with its far-flung, largely fertile territory was granted a series of privileges, from the 1530s onward, which were in line with what would later become the general segregation policy (Gibson 1952, 160f.). In its area, no land grants would be made to non-Indians and no Spaniard or other non-Indian would be allowed to reside in the province (see map 1).

Also, at this early juncture, prior to the enactment of the segregation legislation, the foundation of the city of Puebla to the south of Tlaxcala was motivated by the wish of the authorities that the many vagrants causing the Indians trouble be settled down there (Chevalier 1957). No further measure of that type was taken, however.

A group of scholars who have scrutinized and summarized the records of the Minutes of the Indian Cabildo of Tlaxcala, 1545–1627 (Lockhart, Berdan, and Anderson 1986), make clear that the *cabildo* strongly opposed the presence of "foreigners," that is, both other Indians, such as people from Cholula or Mexico City, and "Spaniards," apart from the local friars and civil functionaries. On 8 August 1550, it declared that "this is the city of us Tlaxtecans only, and the Spaniards are establishing their cities in Mexico City, Puebla and other places."

At this early juncture when the "segregation policy" had not yet been explicitly spelled out, the municipal leaders of Tlaxcala requested and received the support of the viceroy for their policy. Yet, as the same group of scholars explains, the "Indian corporate reaction to Spaniards was not the same as the reaction of individuals making up the corporation" (31). Many individual Indians found it convenient to sell lots and fields to Spaniards and made it possible for a group of Spaniards to emerge within the city who specialized in sheep raising, textiles, transportation, and petty trade. Meanwhile, an official segregation policy became the order of the day in New Spain as such during the 1580s and 1590s. Forceful efforts were made to establish *reducciones,* and non-Indians were to be excluded from them. In the very city of Tlaxcala, in accordance with a 1589 decree, a mestizo by the name of Diego Múnoz de Camargo, who as a spokesman of the city had just obtained at the royal court a number of privileges for Tlaxcala and who was also famous as a local chronicler, would have to leave the city. The decree apparently had no effect, however (Mörner and Gibson 1962). Administrative or judicial procedures were initiated from time to time against non-Indians in various Tlaxcalan towns. But the very fact that at least five *cédulas* were issued to that effect in the case of the same little town, San Francisco de Atexacingo (1587, 1635, 1694, 1735, 1772), eloquently reveals the futility of such efforts. There is also bitterness behind the words of the town's *cabildo* in 1772 about the mestizos, "improperly called *gente de razón*" ("people of reason," as opposed to Indians; see Mörner 1970, 253, 256, 346).

The clear incapacity of the authorities to impose segregation even in a "privileged" Indian territory such as Tlaxcala should be seen against the backdrop of social change. From outside, non-Indians in substantial numbers from the mid-sixteenth century onward settled down there, first in the countryside and the smaller towns, then also in the city of Tlaxcala. At the same time, as everywhere in central New Spain, the Indian population declined rapidly.[2] Non-Indians included farmers and ranchers, as well as merchants and owners of textile sweatshops (*obrajes*). Also, the authorities themselves introduced Spanish administrators side by side with the Indian functionaries (Gibson 1952, 79–88; complemented by Szewczyk 1976). In Gibson's view, nothing else "contributed so directly to the loss of Indian prosperity and prestige in the late sixteenth century as did the steady infiltration of white colonists" (79). This was so regardless of Indian protests, especially because Indian agricultural lands were encroached upon by the cattle of the "Spaniards." The prohibition against Spaniards acquiring land in Tlaxcala, enacted by the king in 1535, was violated by the king himself only three years later by means of a land grant there (Gibson 1952, 80). No wonder that the *cabildo* could not prevent individual Indians from selling their lands to the "Spaniards."

In the early seventeenth century there were no less than 500 non-Indian inhabitants in the city (Mörner 1970, 265). In 1712, there were 94 Spanish haciendas and 85 ranches in the province with a total of 77,000 heads of cattle (González Sánchez 1969). In 1742–43, in addition to 11,000 Indian families in the province of Tlaxcala, there were 800 non-Indian families, no less than 500 in the city itself (Mörner 1970, 268; Trautmann 1981, 95). At the time of Alexander von Humboldt, there were only 900 "pure" Indians left among the 3,400 inhabitants of the city (Mörner 1970, 269). Yet, as Wolfgang Trautmann (1981, 95–103) makes clear, there may have been oscillations over time.[3] Also, basically, as shown by him, non-Indians settled down in villages along the main routes (*caminos reales*). Race mixture through church marriage was especially frequent in the city of Tlaxcala. A sample shows that most Spaniards or mestizos then married Indian women belonging to the traditional elite (*caciques*). In other cases, race mixture was the result of mere cohabitation or promiscuity.

In either case, ethnic duality would persist until the end of the colonial period (and later) in Tlaxcala, where at the same time blacks and mulattoes were strikingly few. In 1810 Indians still formed three-quarters of the population. Apart from the mission districts of Upper California, only the province of Oaxaca in the south harbored a greater Indian majority in the viceroyalty (Mörner 1970, 271). As late as around 1880, about 90 percent of the 225,000 population of the state of Tlaxcala could be classified as "Indians." Moreover, ten years later, according to social anthropologist Hugo Nutini, some 70 percent of the Tlaxcaltecans could only speak Nahuatl, while in the 1970s no more than 3,000 Nahuatl monolinguals remained (1976).

Tunja

In the pleasant highland valleys and green hills of what is now the northern part of the department of Boyacá in Colombia, the Spanish

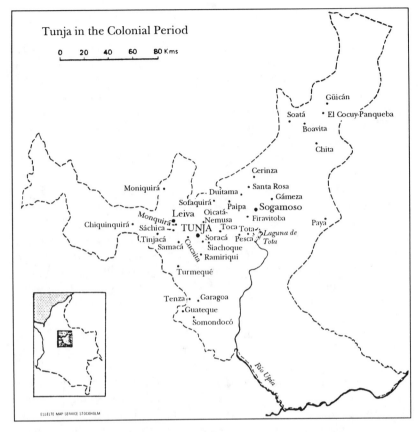

Map 2. Tunja during the Colonial Period.
Source: Mörner 1970, 280

conquistadores of New Granada had founded the city of Tunja in 1539 (see map 2).

Contrary to the region of Tlaxcala, here the Indians were not urbanized but lived in scattered settlements, cultivating the land.[4] They may have comprised nearly 500,000 at the time of contact. By 1565, diseases and other causes had reduced their number to about 100,000, of whom 35,000 were adults liable to pay the headtax (*tributarios*). As everywhere, the *encomenderos* and their foremen were accused of living at the cost of exploiting the Indians harshly. It is a bit ironic that one "Indian" *cacique* who went to Madrid to obtain a royal decree against such abuses in 1578 was himself a mestizo from Turmequé in Tunja (Mörner 1970, 107f.).

Around 1600, like everywhere else in Spanish America, the Indians were forced to settle down in *reducciones* or *resguardos,* as they are consistently called in Colombia. At that time there were 300 "Spanish" citizens in the city of Tunja, a fourth of whom held *encomiendas* with a total of 20,000 tributaries. These "Spaniards" and others had also established numerous *haciendas* in the countryside. Some Indians remained at work on such *haciendas* at least temporarily, while the "Spaniards" leased parts of the *resguardos* to landless mestizos, who rapidly increased in number.

In 1635, an *oidor* (judge) of the *audiencia* of Santa Fé de Bogotá, Juan de Valcarcel, set out on a lengthy inspection tour (*visita*) of fifty-nine Indian communities of the Tunja province. He counted 10,295 Indian tributaries, or a total of 42,295 people. He did not include non-Indians, but there were obviously quite a few. He then seriously tried to implement the segregation laws. In contrast to a previous *oidor,* who in 1593 had simply driven out non-Indians from the Indian pueblos as an administrative measure, Valcarcel took care to launch lawsuits against the infractors of the prohibition, be they *encomenderos,* their foremen, or others. Still, in 1637, in a rather resigned manner, Valcarcel reported that due to the negligence of the *corregidores,* grass-roots–level Spanish administrators, abuses would soon appear again, unless the *corregidores* were strictly controlled. Also, in 1668, the President of New Granada observed that the various *cédulas* imposing segregation had had no effect so far. Notably in the large pueblo of Sogamoso in Tunja, "all kinds of people lived there for good as if it were a Spanish pueblo, sowing the lands of the resguardo on lease" (González 1970, 97).

For more than a century after the *visita* of Valcarcel no similar inspection tour was carried out. When, in 1755, the *oidor* Andrés de Berdugo y Oquendo was given the task, the results revealed that a profound social change had taken place. Now the "Indian" population had shrunk to merely 22,543 individuals, while rural non-Indians (mostly mestizos) by now formed a total of no less than 37,685—that is, a sheer majority in most pueblos.

Rather than Indian biological decline, racial and cultural mixture were probably responsible for this process of change. Moreover, the Indians now often lived once again dispersed, while non-whites, *vecinos* as they were called, lived in the centers of the old *resguardos.* The Indians no longer spoke their Chibcha language as they did in the 1630s. One can hardly blame Berdugo for finding the segregation laws hard or impossible to apply in the sense they had been intended to be. In his desire to provide the landless mestizo settlers with land, he began to apply, cautiously, the segregation legislation in reverse. In some pueblos where the remaining Indians were few, the *resguardo* was dissolved, its lands auctioned out and the Indians forcefully transferred to pueblos that still retained their Indian character. But they were not, at least in practice, assured full participation in their new pueblo but merely added to it as a category of *agregados* with inferior land or none at all at their disposal. With a regalist interpretation, the authorities claimed that Indians had never received their original lands with *pleno dominio* but merely in usufruct.

In the 1770s, Francisco Antonio Moreno y Escandón, a distinguished administrator, himself a New Granadian, made a profound analysis of the problem. He found that the Indians often preferred to work for pay with nearby *hacendados* while letting out their own lands to landless mestizos. He thought the time was ripe for the whole system of Indian tribute and segregation to vanish to let the Indians instead "hispanize" themselves. Yet, the law still dictated separation. Moreno and another functionary of the *audiencia* therefore went on extinguishing *resguardos*, auctioning out the land to the highest bidder—often a *hacendado* rather than a *vecino* peasant—and transferring smaller groups of Indians from one pueblo to another. To take Sogamoso as an example, once again, non-Indians by now numbered a total of 1,810 people, whereas the Indians were only 589 (including 79 tributaries). Under these conditions, Moreno forced them to be transferred to another pueblo, Paipa, with about 1,000 Indians. The sale of the *resguardos* of the Sogamoso district eventually brought a total of 20,035 pesos to the royal treasury. Less than half of the area was acquired by local residents (Meza Lopehandía 1976, 212). However, the new regent of the *audiencia*, Juan Francisco Gutiérrez de Piñeres, proved to be opposed to Moreno's way of carrying out segregation policy. He preferred, simply, to have the process of assimilation continue where mixture was already a fact. Where Indians still remained isolated, on the other hand, their usufruct of the remaining community lands should be defended (Phelan 1978, 92).

Cohabitation of Indians and non-Indians appears usually to have been full of tensions and conflicts. The Corregidor of Sogamoso, for example, in 1765 pointed out that segregation was needed to free the *vecinos* from Indian threats! Seven years later, some 400 Indians attacked the house and mill of a local *vecino*, stripped his wife of her clothing, and expelled her from the *resguardo* (McFarlane 1984, 33f.).

Even so, McFarlane is right that for long the "the hemmorhage of Indian communities through the processes of migration and miscegenation [had] weakened their capacity for resistance" (34).

Thus, the massive Comunero movement of 1781 was triggered by other reasons and mostly recruited among the humble mestizo peasants who had been favored by Moreno y Escandón. Among their wishes, naturally, was to keep the *resguardo* land they had already acquired and, if possible, to acquire more. Yet, there was also an Indian element in the uprising, and many Indians had suffered severely from the enforced transfers of the 1770s (see, e.g., König 1988, 79). Their leader was Ambrosio Pisco, like Tupac Amaro II in Peru, a mestizo claiming to be a descendant of preconquest royalty. Unlike him, however, as John Phelan underscores, Pisco had shown no concern for Indian affairs prior to 1781. Instead, as a businessman he had acquired a considerable fortune and only reluctantly joined the Comunero rebellion. The embittered Indians, however, enthusiastically greeted him as a savior. As Phelan sees it, the Comunero leaders put him to a double use. First, he helped to restrain the violence of the Indian rebels. Second, through him and 5,000 angry Indians, armed pressure was exerted on Bogotá. This helped to produce the compromise agreement with the authorities known as "Capitulaciones de Zipaquirá," concluded on 5 June 1781. These included an important clause (section 7) on the *resguardos:* The Indians "should be restored to the lands that they possessed since time immemorial. The *resguardos* that they now hold should be theirs not only in usufruct but also as full owners[5] and be their property to dispose of and sell as they see fit as owners."

I believe that John Phelan is quite right when he says, "The last sentence is the key" to the interpretations of this ambivalent formulation. The Indians should be given a title in fee simple to their common lands in order to be able to sell them to the mestizos. The "restoration" was not seriously meant.

On the other hand, the other party in Zipaquirá, Antonio Caballero y Góngora, Archbishop and Acting Viceroy, apparently followed the policy of Gutiérrez de Piñeres. The Indians should enjoy usufruct to their lands, and thus be unable to sell them. After the Capitulaciones had been undone, this policy would be the prevailing one until the end of the colonial era, even though some small-scale restorations also took place. We do know, for instance, that Indians in the Sogamoso district got some *resguardos* back.[6] Yet, what had happened during more than a century and had been confirmed by men like Moreno y Escandón could not be undone. The rural structure and ethnicity of the highland provinces of Nueva Granada/Colombia had been profoundly altered.

By far the majority of the rural masses were mestizo. Even so, legal documentation shows that appeals sometimes continued to be made to the obsolete laws of segregation, in one case in 1808 by a priest who wanted to get rid of some parishioners (Mörner 1970, 356f.), in another case, in 1807, with respect to *vecinos* in Paipa, the pueblo where the Indians of Sogamoso had been forced to settle down almost thirty years earlier (Mörner 1963, 81).

Yet, the right of non-Indians to live among them, provided that they paid their rents and did no harm to the Indians, was not explicitly recognized in law by the national state until 4 October 1821.

The Guaraní Missions

What happened in the populous Guaraní missions under Jesuit administration, in both ecclesiastical and secular affairs, in the eastern part of Rio de la Plata is very different, indeed, from the failure of imposing segregation in nuclear areas, such as Tlaxcala and Tunja (see map 3).

The Jesuit application of segregation legislation was not blind, however, but dictated by what Jesuit leaders found that their missions needed.

In the early 1600s, temporary visits of foreign travelers were allowed, even if the Father Provincial in 1609 instructed the missionaries to try to avoid such visits. Toward the end of the century, with the blessing of the Father General in Rome, the Provincial made clear that temporary visits should not exceed three days. That was in keeping with the general legislation. However, in the early 1720s, according to the orders issued by the Provincial, at first just two, later six of the thirty missions would be allowed to receive any outside visitors at all. Mostly merchants, the visitors would then be housed at a special inn, being kept as isolated as possible from the Indians and above all from their women. Circumstances make clear that Jesuits did only receive visitors in the six "Pueblos de Abajo," the ones closest to Paraguay, for trade reasons. Yet, the Jesuit policy of keeping twenty-four of their Guaraní missions closed to foreign visitors enjoyed no explicit support in the general legislation, even if it might have been in keeping with its spirit. The acute conflicts with Paraguayan settlers at this time help to explain the Jesuit attitude. At the same time, on the southern frontier of the mission area, non-Indian vagrants were roaming around on the Pampas, forefathers of the *gauchos,* and it is not surprising that they were far from welcome to visit the missions.

The prohibition of non-Indian permanent residence among the

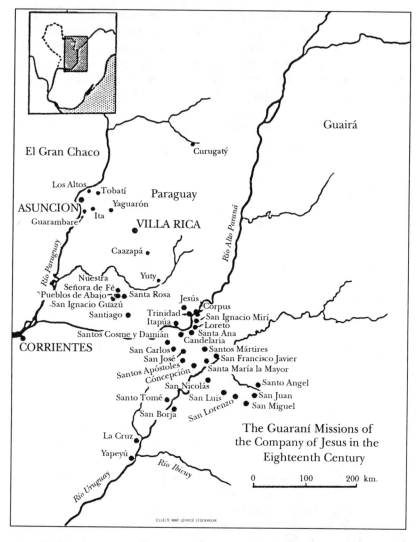

El Gran Chaco

Guairá

Curugatý

Paraguay

Los Altos
Tobatí
ASUNCION
Yaguarón
Guarambare
Ita
VILLA RICA

Caazapá

Nuestra
Señora de Fé
Pueblos de Abajo
San Ignacio Guazú
Santiago
Santa Rosa
Yuty

Jesús
Corpus
Trinidad
San Ignacio Mirí
Itapúa
Loreto
Santos Cosme y Damián
Santa Ana
Candelaria

CORRIENTES
San Carlos
Santos Mártires
San José
San Francisco Javier
Santos Apóstoles
Concepción
Santa María la Mayor

San Nicolás
Santo Angel

Santo Tomé
San Luis
San Juan
San Borja
San Lorenzo
San Miguel

La Cruz

Yapeyú

Río Ibicuy

Río Uruguay

Río Paraguay

Río Alto Paraná

The Guaraní Missions of
the Company of Jesus in the
Eighteenth Century

0   100   200 km.

ESSELTE MAP SERVICE STOCKHOLM

Map 3. The Guaraní Missions of the Jesuits in the Eighteenth Century. The *pueblos de Abajo* (villages down to the South—obviously a Paraguayan expression) that received visitors were Nuestra Señora de Fé, San Ignacio Guazú, Santiago, Santa Rosa, Santos Cosme y Damián, and Itapúa.
Source: Mörner 1970, 321

Indians in their pueblos was, as we have seen, very strictly forbidden in general legislation. Moreover, when this prohibition was specifically decreed in the River Plata provinces in 1611 by the *oidor* Francisco de Alfaro, we know that he was actually very much under Jesuit influence (Mörner 1968, 37ff., 172). In 1681, the segregation laws were included in the Recopilación. Thus, their application in the Guaraní missions should not make us raise an eyebrow.

On the other hand, it is indeed noteworthy that the Jesuits did allow a rather important exception. Once again, their pragmatic view of what the missions really needed prevailed. Until the early 1730s, the missions' supply of meat, which had become a staple food for the Indians, had been satisfied by the enormous herds of wild cattle roaming around in present-day Uruguay, Vaquería del Mar, and to the east of the missions, Vaquería de los Pinares. Due to increasing competition with Spaniards from Santa Fé and Portuguese from the east or from the bulwark of Colonia do Sacramento on the seashore, this apparently boundless free resource had been exhausted by 1730. The Jesuit leaders of the Guaraní community had to establish their own *estancias* closer to the missions. This required an amount of know-how that the Indians, perhaps even the Jesuits, did not possess. Consequently, in 1735 the Provincial and his main advisors decided explicitly to allow that some "Spanish" and mestizo *estancieros* should be invited to instruct the Indians in their new task.

It is worthwhile to keep in mind that the missions had reached their demographic peak in 1732 with no less than 141,182 Indians, according to the exceptionally reliable yearly population records available. This peak, however, was followed by a drastic drop to merely 73,910 in 1740. Historical demographer Ernesto Maeder (1989) believes that this should be attributed to a combination of lengthy mobilization of Indian men against the Paraguayan rebels, famine, and epidemics. Clearly, the meat supply had become more crucial than ever. One of the Jesuit missionaries, José Cardiel, in a report from 1758, names five outside *estancieros* who, under contract for a number of years, had settled down in the pueblos with their families. This was so notwithstanding the fact that, as Cardiel admits, a royal *cédula* forbade such residence. In another report from 1747, Cardiel also testifies to the difficulties these Spanish "foremen" had in getting along with their Indian "pupils."

After the Jesuit expulsion in 1767–68, the exclusion of the non-Indians was suspended by Governor Francisco de Paula Bucareli. He openly wanted some Spaniards to settle down in the pueblos "to facilitate reciprocal trade whereby, together with communication, the Indians become civilized as we want them to be." At the same time, new secular administrators together with new priests took over the task of the Jesuits. A general decay now set in, though not as quickly as historians used to believe. From 88,828 people in 1768, the population shrank to 56,092 in 1783 and 45,720 in 1797. That last year, another governor once again forbade the permanent residence of non-Indians in the pueblos because of the many abuses they had committed. Not more than three days at a time (Mörner 1970, 322f.)! But this attempt to revive the segregation policy probably had no effect whatsoever. Maeder attributes the final decline of the Guaraní pueblos to excessive work, malnutrition, and epidemics as well as to desertions. The latter involved rural work in the surrounding areas and *mestizaje* there. The previous isolationist policy had not protected the pueblos from epidemics. This much is clear from the high incidence of epidemics over the years, particularly in 1733–40. On the other hand, until 1768, it did prevent the process of Indian integration with other rural inhabitants which had set in so much sooner, for instance, in Tlaxcala and Tunja.

CHAPTER 4

Dark-skinned New "Citizens" Face the Newborn National State

Early National Venezuela

THE CITIES where viceroys or captains general resided would be the sites for the Spanish American revolts against traditional colonial rule in 1810. To extend a city's jurisdiction over that of other cities became a key problem for early revolutionary governments. This is why Venezuela, the first country to enact a constitution of its own, chose a federal model in 1811, inspired by the U.S. Constitution. However, the early collapse of the Republic could be blamed precisely on its loose decentralized structure, as Simón Bolívar would be the first to assert. Instead, Bolívar's constitutions for Gran Colombia (1819, 1821) were highly centralized.

When breaking loose from Gran Colombia in 1830 under the leadership of a forceful, pragmatic *caudillo,* José Antonio Páez, Venezuelans opted for a model said to be "centro-federal." To be sure, the provinces had elected provincial assemblies, but the governors were named by the president, and the national state was a unitary one. This constitution survived until 1857; that period from 1830 to 1857 is the one we are mainly looking at here. The period is divided into two very different phases. The era dominated by Páez, that is until 1848, is known in historiography as the "conservative oligarchy."[1] It is followed by the era dominated by the Monagas brothers as national *caudillos*—the "liberal oligarchy," as it is usually called. They saw fit to launch a new, in fact centralist constitution in 1857, adorned with universal suffrage for men and some municipal—instead of provincial—autonomy. As early as 1858, however, another constitution implied a return to the 1830 model. It was not until 1864, that is, after the bloody, so-called Federal War (1859–63), that a federal constitution like that of 1811 was enacted. Even though "federation" was a cherished war slogan, it probably had little real meaning. This is, at least, what Antonio Leocadio Guzmán, a leading liberal politician, cynically admitted in 1867. When the drafters of the Constitution of 1857 did not make it "federal," Guzmán and his friends did so, "as every revolution needs a banner." But if the others had said "federation," "we would have said 'centralization' instead." Moreover, in fact, from Guzmán's son Antonio Guzmán Blanco (1870–88) onward, national *caudillo* rule became increasingly harsh and effective (until 1935), so that constitutional niceties such as federalism lost whatever substance they ever had.

It is hardly surprising that, prior to 1857, franchise was strictly limited to a minority of the free male population, on the basis of wealth and literacy. In 1830, property producing a rent of 50 pesos, an annual income of 100 pesos, or a salary of 150 pesos was required for the right to vote, and servants were excluded (Gil Fortoul 1954, 3:351f.). The economic qualifications required for electors (popularly elected to choose the president and vice-president as well as members of Congress) and for the members of Congress themselves were considerably higher.[2] In 1846, out of a total of 1.3 million inhabitants, a tenth of them were qualified to vote. Partly due to the unrest, only half of them did so. There could have been almost 9,000 electors, but in fact only 342 cast their votes (Gil Fortoul 1954, 2:276f.).[3] Democratization was sudden, in 1857–58. In the 1858 Constitution, even the literacy requirement was abolished. Four years earlier, slavery had also finally been abolished. The question that remained was, of course, if elections would really matter. From 1846 onward, politics on a national level in Venezuela had turned increasingly violent.

Behind this violence was a series of structural factors. First, by 1810 some 60,000 slaves, used primarily in cocoa plantations, formed almost 9 percent of the total population, an unusually high share in Spanish American terms. Even more numerous were persons of mixed race, here called *pardos* whether mulattoes, zamboes, or, at times, mestizos.[4] In the late eighteenth century, some of them had become both literate and wealthy. This merely increased the discrimination against them on the part of the white elite. Thus, the so-called Regimen de Castas, or colonial social hierarchy of Spanish America, with the whites on the top became especially repressive in Venezuela, it seems, because the linkage between color and slavery was so strong.

Behind the coast and coastal ranges where plantations thrived and urban centers had grown up, the immense plains of the interior (the llanos) formed a very fluid frontier area used for ranching. Its tough, independent-minded population grew little by little, thanks to deserted slaves and other marginal elements from the nuclear areas. The llaneros (the cattle hands) detested the white coastal elite, whether Spaniards or criollos. As the latter launched the 1810 revolution, Tomás Boves who, though an Asturian himself, had become their charismatic leader, crushed the criollo rebels with the help of his llanero warriors. Some years later, Páez, who had grown up a llanero, was able to repeat the performance but now the white loyalist elite was crushed, instead.[5] More than a decade of savage warfare made the cost of independence in Venezuela especially heavy in both human and material terms. Geographer Augustín Codazzi estimated Venezuela's population in 1840 at 950,000. In his view, this was a third less than it would have been without the war.[6]

As far as the Indians were concerned, who lived in missions with common landholdings (*resguardos*) in various parts of the country, a very fateful political decision was taken in the wake of Independence. On 4 October 1821 a law was enacted that abolished Indian tribute and decreed an individualization of the *resguardos*. The law was well meant, of course. The Indians should be transformed into land-holding peasants of the European type. But those to benefit from the measure were primarily non-Indian large landholders who were quick to acquire the individual parcels (Izard 1979a, 52f.).

The War for Independence eliminated the legal discrimination against free persons of color. This means that socioracial designations would no longer be given in the censuses. Nevertheless, in 1841 Codazzi ventured to estimate that whites were 28 percent, racially mixed people were 44 percent, and slaves were 5 percent of the population; Indians of various degrees would make up the remaining 23 percent. Independence also dealt slavery a decisive blow.[7] Some 40,000 slaves were still left, but according to a decision in 1821, no more slaves would be born in or imported to the country. The children of the slaves would instead be submitted to an "apprentice" work period under the owners of their mothers. Yet, for reasons analyzed in detail by John Lombardi (1971), the final emancipation of the 12,000 slaves and the 11,000 "apprentices" did not take place until 1854.

While cocoa production languished, traditionally slave-based as it was, a virtual coffee boom took place in the 1830s and early 1840s. External demand also caused a fourfold increase in the export of cattle hides from the llanos between 1840 and 1855. Economic expansion was conditioned by easy credits from abroad. They were guaranteed by the government from 1834 onward. Yet, when in the early 1840s coffee prices dropped, landowners were severely affected. At the same time, they experienced a crucial lack of labor when *jornaleros* made clear they preferred subsistence agriculture to lower wages. This is the general background of the sociopolitical crisis of the latter 1840s.[8]

The elite hoped to resolve the lack of labor through white immigration. It should be kept in mind that even in colonial times a large number of the whites were poor, so-called *blancos de orilla,* and often from the Canary Islands. From 1830 to 1845, Venezuela attracted as many as 12,000 immigrants from the Canaries. The political instability which followed, however, reduced immigration to a trickle.

From 1840 onward, the elite had split over mainly questions of finance and credit. The commercial interests around Páez were challenged by a Liberal Party consisting mostly of indebted landowners. Under the surface neither Conservatives nor Liberals cared about the rural smallholders/day laborers. No clear borderline can be drawn between the latter two groups. Both suffered keenly from "debt slavery" and other obligations or restrictions on their freedom imposed by the large landowners. The ethnic conflicts of colonial times were revitalized.[9] The elite was still overwhelmingly white, to some extent of old aristocratic families *(godos).*[10] Most of the poor, on the other hand, were more or less dark-skinned.

Together, downward business trends in the 1840s and late 1850s and the political division of the white elite would lead to a sociopolitical explosion, the Guerra Federal (1859–63).[11] On the eve of the war, Venezuela had 1,560,000 inhabitants. According to Brito Figueroa (1975, 455), no fewer than 200,000 perished in the course of the war. In this way, it is often claimed, ethnic conflicts were finally lessened in Venezuelan society.[12]

The various issues I have just touched upon have been intelligently discussed by scholars such as John Lombardi, Brito Figueroa, Miguel Izard, and Robert Paul Matthews. Yet these same issues remain somewhat enigmatic. My plan is to discuss them here with reference to three different Venezuelan provinces. We must keep in mind that the provinces of the period did not coincide with the various natural regions that are characteristic of the country and that were the basis for rural production (see maps 4, 5).

Provinces stretched from the humid, hot coastal strip over the more fresh coastal range down to the llanos. What determined the socioeconomic setup of a province, then, were the environmental proportions. Politics was concentrated in the provincial capital. However, the domination of the national capital, Caracas, backed up as it was by a province that was by far the most populous and wealthy in the country, was never in dispute. Yet, the fact of having access to government in Caracas might give influence to one or another provincial elite group. As Lombardi puts it, the Federal War did not concern "any abstract principle of states' rights but only the opportunity to con-

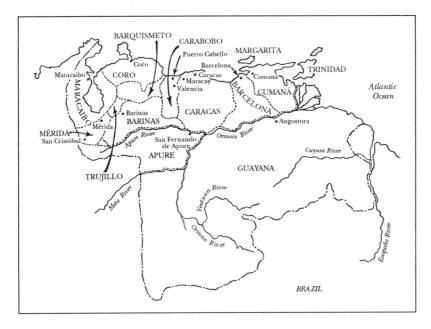

Map 4. Venezuela in 1840: Provinces.
Source: Lombardi 1971, 4

trol the apparatus of Caracas, the bureaucratic and institutional capital."[13]

I shall focus on the problems of power in the Venezuelan Republic. What power was actually displayed by the state on the provincial level? What was the relationship between the elites and the masses on that very level? How did the dark-skinned masses express their frustrations when the formal abolition of the discrimination inherent in the colonial caste society appeared to have had little impact on social reality?

Cumaná, Land of Earthquakes and *Caudillo* Stability

Founded as early as 1520, the city of Cumaná had been the traditional center of the whole "Oriente" of Venezuela, even though the Island of Margarita and the llano province of Barcelona were usually administered separately.

In 1761, Governor Diguja, on his visit to the province of New Andalucia (Cumaná), found a total of 12,163 (non-Indian) inhabitants, to which an estimated 10,000 Indians gathered in missions and Indian

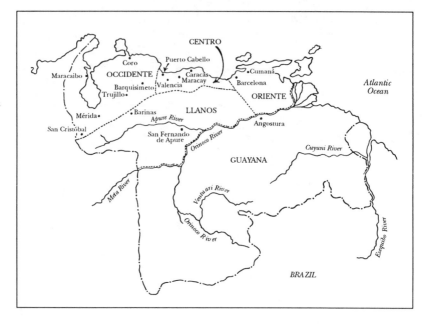

Map 5. Venezuela in 1840: Major Geopolitical Regions.
Source: Lombardi 1971, 5

parishes (*doctrinas*) in the interior could be added. In his data, an elite of some 1,000 members of noble families can be discerned, but their wealth appears to have been modest. There were about five times as many poor whites and mulattoes (*pardos*). They were fishermen, contrabandists, and so forth. Probably no more than 2,000 slaves were concentrated on seventy-six cocoa plantations, the main staple of the province and all of Venezuela at the time. By far most of that production, thanks to the Dutch, was exported as contraband, as even the governor himself admitted. Among other products, cotton should also be mentioned. Since the late eighteenth century, it was being produced here as well as in, for instance, Valencia (the later province of Carabobo). But thanks to better purifying techniques, the cotton of Cumaná seems to have enjoyed a better price abroad. This export of a raw material in demand forms at least one direct link to early European industrialization, in Catalogne as well as Britain (Izard 1979a, 72).

Foreign visitors such as Alexander von Humboldt in 1800, François Depons in 1802, and J. J. Dauxion Lavaisse in 1807 all found the city of Cumaná and its surroundings unusually pleasant. They noticed the havoc caused by the earthquake of 1797, but their data suggest rapid population growth and economic expansion. According to Dauxion, the province had 68,000 people, the capital no less than 28,000. Humboldt, on the other hand, found such figures to be inflated. The city would have 16,800 inhabitants at most, he wrote. In 1793, the provincial government prepared a survey of annual per capita commercial consumption, by class, of Cumaná. As expected, the white elite composed just over 1 percent of the non-Indian population (average: 102 pesos). However, an upper-middle-class group of 3,659 persons "of whatever hierarchy and color with what is required to maintain oneself in decency" composed another 8.4 percent of the 43,468 non-Indian inhabitants, according to that estimate (average: 57 pesos). That group was rather closely followed by a group of other free people—soldiers, small farmers, artisans—who composed 18.5 percent (average: 39 pesos). The two bottom strata (31,000), characterized as "poor," composed the remaining 71 percent. Even so, not only dayworkers but also slaves were placed in the higher bracket (average: 8 pesos). The foreign visitors agree that commerce was entirely controlled by Catalan merchants.[14]

We should not forget that in the backlands of Cumaná and its sister city Barcelona there were rather large Indian missions, first established by Franciscan and Capuchin friars in the 1660s. Around 1800, according to Alexander von Humboldt, there were 15,000 Indians in the missions of Caripe, Cumaná, and 24,700 in those of Píritu, Barcelona. But Humboldt also observed that they were being increasingly invaded by non-Indians and losing their character as missions. The Indians even began to forget their mother tongues. Thus, these missions, as we can see, were quite different from those of the Jesuits in the River Plate—that is, until 1767–68 (Mörner 1970, 326–32).

The struggle for independence in the Oriente had three special characteristics. First, it was led by leaders who only grudgingly recognized the leading part played by Caracas and Bolívar. The main actor of the East was General Santiago Mariño (1788–1854). Second, the struggle, even in Venezuelan terms, was unusually destructive. According to a report from the early 1820s, "all the cocoa plantations of this Department are almost destroyed." And third, the Minister of Finance of Gran Colombia affirmed that Cumaná was then one of the provinces of the Republic lagging most behind. Its agriculture had also suffered from price fall (Izard 1972, 41f., 58). In 1830, Cumaná's population seems to have shrunk to merely 52,000 people.

Recovering steadily to 74,400 inhabitants in 1844, Cumaná showed considerable demographic vigor (see tables 1–2).

Region and State in Latin America's Past

Table 1. The Population of Venezuela, 1839: Barinas, Carabobo, and Cumaná

Province and Cantones	Population	Men Fit for Military Service	Slaves	Export Crops
Barinas:				
Barinas	11,297	1,200	187	Cocoa, indigo, coffee, sugar, tobacco
Obispo	21,101	1,900	234	Cocoa, indigo, coffee, sugar, tobacco
Pedraza	5,212	500	38	Cocoa, coffee
Ospino	10,208	1,000	197	Cocoa, coffee
Nutrias	13,620	1,600	148	Sugar, cocoa, cotton, indigo
Guanare	28,398	2,600	489	Cocoa, indigo, coffee, sugar, tobacco
Araure	15,073	1,800	148	Cocoa, coffee, cotton, sugar, indigo
Guanarito	4,588	500	17	Sugar, indigo, cotton
Total (62 parishes):	109,497	11,100	1,458[a]	
Carabobo:				
Valencia	40,323	2,800	1,969	Coffee, cocoa, indigo, tobacco, sugar, cotton
Puerto Cabello	6,189	600	424	Cocoa, coffee, sugar
San Carlos	21,829	1,600	758	Cocoa, sugar
Nirgua	6,539	700	30	Cocoa, coffee, sugar
Pao	13,414	1,300	130	Sugar
Montalbán	5,836	600	267	Cocoa, coffee, sugar
Ocumare	2,847	200	886	Cocoa, coffee
Total (53 parishes)	96,977	6,800	4,460[a]	
Cumaná:				
Cumaná	9,093	700	298	Cocoa, sugar, cotton, coconuts
Cumanacoa	3,189	200	24	Sugar, cotton, tobacco
Aragua	5,485	500	23	Sugar, coffee, cotton, tobacco, cocoa
Maturín	7,861	700	121	Cocoa, coffee, sugar, cotton
Caños/Barrancas	4,000	400	87	Sugar
Güiria	1,918	150	198	Cocoa, coffee
Rio Caribe	4,749	250	408	Cocoa, coffee, sugar

Province and Cantones	Population	Men Fit for Military Service	Slaves	Export Crops
Carúpano	9,387	800	159	Cocoa, coffee, sugar, cotton
Cariaco	4,989	500	163	Cocoa, coffee, sugar, cotton, tobacco
Total (48 parishes)	50,676	4,200	1,481[a]	
Republic	945,548		49,782[a]	

Note: [a]The number of slaves can be expressed as a percentage of the total population: for Barinas, 1.3 percent; for Carabobo, 4.5 percent; for Cumaná, 2.9 percent; and for the Republic, 5.3 percent.

Source: Codazzi 1841, 522f. (Barinas), 406f. (Carabobo), 586f. (Cumaná), 244 (Republic). By 1840, Codazzi estimated the number of free Indians at 52,000. In 1825, according to Codazzi, Barinas had 87,179 people, Carabobo, 74,317, and Cumaná, 35,174; present Venezuela, 701,635. Codazzi (1841, 575) says Cumaná has 8 cantones but lists 9 (including Caños/Barrancas, which, according to Landaeta Rosales [1963, 1:93] was part of Maturín). According to Lombardi, Codazzi's slave figures "apparently include the free-born manumisos" (Lombardi 1971, 122–27 and 162).

Yet smaller districts and towns such as Carúpano and Maturín were responsible for this growth rather than the capital (Memorias 1973, 129). In 1852, a new visitor, Brazilian diplomat Lisboa, found Cumaná the most pleasant place he had seen in Venezuela (Lisboa 1954, 161). It had no more than six or seven thousand inhabitants, however (157). The stagnation of the city may have had to do with an earthquake in 1839. In the same year, geographer Codazzi thought that some 45 percent of the Cumanese were active in agriculture, 25 percent in ranching, and the rest in manufacturing and other occupations. In 1846, Codazzi underscores the good location of Cumaná and its immediate hinterland for its exports, even though some of the roads were poor (1960, 2:184f.).

There is much to suggest that social control in Cumaná remained firmly in the hands of the traditional elite and Mariño, even though he spent the years 1836–45 in exile. Likewise, Barcelona was controlled by the *caudillo* José Tadeo Monagas and his cattle baron family. This is strikingly shown by the extraordinary distribution of state lands (*baldíos*) in these two provinces precisely by virtue of the law enacted on 10 April 1848 at the end of the Monagas domination of national govern-

Region and State in Latin America's Past

Table 2. The Population of Venezuela, 1854–1873: Barinas, Carabobo, and Cumaná

Province and Cantones	1854	Province and Cantones (New Name)	1873
Barinas:		Zamora:	
Barinas	14,023	Barinas	11,563
Obispo	13,083	Obispo	10,155
Pedraza	6,452	Pedraza	8,270
Libertad	10,980	Rojas	11,084
Nutrias	11,702	Nutrias	12,412
		Oriental	5,965
Total (5 cantones,		Total (6 departments,	
40 parishes):	56,242[a]	35 districts):	59,449
Carabobo:			
Valencia	66,277	Valencia	61,696
Puerto Cabello	11,387	Puerto Cabello	14,273
San Carlos	31,523	[part of the state of Cojedes]	
Nirgua	38,045	[part of the state of Yaracuy]	
Pao	38,643	[part of the state of Cojedes]	
Montalbán	20,714	Montalbán	12,425
		(part of Cojedes)	
Ocumare de la Costa	3,214	Ocumare de la Costa	3,890
Tinaco	20,706	[part of the state of Cojedes]	
		Bejuma	11,454
		Guacara	3,407
		[To be added	460]
Total (8 cantones,		Total (6 departments,	
40 parishes):	230,509[b]	29 parishes):	117,605
Cumaná:		Sucre:	
Cumaná	14,216	Sucre	16,656
Cumanacoa	4,695	Montes	5,636
Aragua	7,609	[part of the state of Maturín]	
Maturín	14,323	[part of the state of Maturín]	
Caños	3,857		
Güiria	3,193	Mariño	6,705
Río Caribe	6,962	Arismendi	8,568
Carúpano	14,771	Bermúdez	18,392
Cariaco	6,202	Rivero	6,224
Total (9 cantones,		Total (6 departments,	
46 parishes):	75,828[c]	8 municipalities):	62,181
Republic			
Total (16 provinces, 96 cantones,		Total (20 states, 1 federal district,	
560 parishes):	1,560,433	126 departments):	1,784,194

ment. Out of total distribution of 297 *leguas cuadradas,* Barcelona was responsible for 44 percent, Cumaná for 21 percent (Materiales 1971, lix). Almost all of this enormous amount of land fell to members of the Monagas family and their close clients (ibid., lxvi–lxviii). Moreover, the decline of slavery in Cumaná was remarkably slow. From 1,400 slaves in 1830, the final abolition in 1854, enacted by the younger Monagas brother, José Gregorio, freed as many as 1,100 with due compensation of 85,600,000 pesos to their elite owners. Also, as already touched upon, during the Monagas decade, the mildly liberal elite of the Oriente had privileged access to national political and administrative positions in Caracas. During a period when Venezuela in general experienced increasing unrest (1846–58), Cumaná remained relatively calm.[15] Although an anti-white rising was reported in 1837–38, it seems to have been marginal (Izard 1981, 129).

At the same time, Cumaná seems to have been the cradle of post-1830 federalism, elsewhere suddenly thrown into the political scene during the 1859–63 civil war. Interestingly, José Tadeo Monagas and Mariño in 1831 already had agreed upon the formation of the Oriente as a separate state, directly placed under the President of Venezuela. Mariño apparently had let himself be manipulated by the more astute Monagas. The national *caudillo,* Páez, was horrified, however, when he heard about that idea (Castillo Blomquist 1987, 29). In 1849, the political leaders of Cumaná pleaded to Congress for greater provincial autonomy. They referred especially to the lack of provincial benefits from foreign trade. They also demanded direct universal suffrage and the abolition of slavery. In 1853, disgusted with the chilly attitude of the administration and Congress and the bad state of national finances, they passed from words to action (Matthews 1977, 134). Cumaná was

---

Notes: [a] It should be noted that the cantones of Guanare, Ospino, Araure, and Guanarito, included in Barinas as of 1839, now formed a province of their own, Portuguesa. This largely explains the 50 percent "reduction" of the population.

[b] In 1856, the cantones of San Carlos, Tinaco, Pao, and Girardot were broken out to form the province of Cojedes.

[c] In 1856, the cantones of Maturín, Aragua, and Bermúdez were broken out to form the province of Maturín.

Sources: For 1854, same as table 1; for 1873, Tejera (1986, 1–2).

not the only province to rise in that year but its case had special characteristics. The rebellion on the fourth of June was led by the governor himself, Colonel José Guevara, and most participants were recruited among regular and militia military forces. Guevara proclaimed a federal system and all the districts (*cantones*) joined in this decision.[16] Counterforces led by General Gerardo Monagas were on their way to crush the rebels, when nature chose to anticipate their move. On 15 July, a terrible earthquake destroyed the city of Cumaná, killing, among others, the commander of the revolutionary forces and two hundred of his men. Now pacification was easy (González Guinan 1954, 5:299–304).

It should be noted that at the Constitutional Convention in Valencia in 1858, it was Cumaná deputies who defended the adoption of a purely federal system. They were overwhelmingly defeated, however, especially after a brilliant speech by conservative Fermín Toro. Admittedly, on the theoretical level, Toro found federalism to be "the most perfect one until now of politicial institutions." Yet, the backward state of rural Venezuela at the time made it unworkable, he realistically argued.

Cumaná had its share of the destructive violence of the protracted Federal War. Federation was proclaimed there in August 1859. A few months later, Cumaná, with its 76,000 people, was under the control of federal troops (Brito Figueroa 1975, 434).[17] Yet, in the course of the war, it became clear that the weight of violence and political power had shifted westward, as Lombardi underscores (1985, 200). In the early 1870s, the all-important coffee production had followed suit (Izard 1973). In the state of Sucre (Cumaná), landholding remained very uneven. In 1950, of a total of 19,832 agricultural holdings, only 45 percent of the landholders cultivated their own land (Vila 1965, 190).

In a comparative perspective, Cumaná, like Barcelona prior to the Federal War, had enjoyed relatively stable *caudillo* rule and had been relatively free in its relationship with Caracas. The masses were under elite control. The dark-skinned new "citizens" constituted no major problem. Probably due mainly to the traditions of the War of Independence, federalism was espoused by the provincial elite rather early.

Carabobo, Land of Glory and Slaves

Carabobo was named after Bolívar's decisive victory, which took place in the province in 1821. Its main city, Valencia, and its main port, Puerto Cabello, had been centers of the western part of Central Venezuela since the sixteenth century. In 1812, under the First Republic,

Valencia even served as a national capital. François Depons (1960) tells us the nice story that the aristocratic criollos of Valencia used to be haughty, lazy, and poor. However, sometime in the late colonial era, when ordered by a military commander to cultivate a plot of land each, to assure the food supply, they found agriculture quite interesting.

Thus, by the early 1800s, the city had become quite prosperous. Situated as a crossing point between Caracas, the llanos, and the Andean region, its location was excellent. Moreover, Valencia was closely linked to Puerto Cabello, an excellent natural harbor but unfortunately riddled with fevers. By 1800, a third of the exports via Puerto Cabello was reputed to have been legal, another third illegal and bound for Curaçao, while the last third, also illegal, went to Jamaica. In addition to mules from the southern llanos, cocoa and cotton were the staples of the export trade. Cocoa was primarily produced on the humid coast and on adjacent mountain slopes. Otherwise, the highland basin around Lake Valencia, which its province shared with the Maracay district of the Caracas province, was the main agricultural area.

Not surprisingly, slaves in the province later to be called Carabobo were numerous. A visiting bishop (1773–82) found 2,516 slaves out of a total population of 17,352 (slaves were 15 percent of the population; see Vila 1966, 103f.).[18] Remarkably, we notice that in six out of nineteen parishes, the number of slaves even increased between 1800 and 1820, the wars notwithstanding (Lombardi 1976, vol. 2, table 1). From a peak of 4,700 in 1830, the slave population sank slowly to 3,200 in 1844 and to 2,800 on the eve of final abolition in 1854 (Materiales 1979, 533). Another set of data gives 1881 slaves and 1764 *manumisos* (apprentices) set free by the abolition law. If so, Carabobo was next in number of slaves to the much larger Caracas province. As far as the process of settlement is concerned, out of some twenty parish seats in 1800, six are said to have been originally established by landowners for their slaves, while two had been originally Indian *reducciones*. The Wars of Independence no doubt brought the province both human losses and material destruction. Especially on the coast, some parishes lost population between 1800 and 1819/20. On the provincial level, after the start of a period of peace, demographic growth was quite good, from 74,000 in 1825 to nearly 97,000 in 1839, that is, by 30 percent in fourteen years (see table 1). Economically, by 1873, together with the two Andean states, Carabobo was the leading producer of coffee, by then the most important staple of the Republic (Izard 1973).

There is much to suggest that social conflicts in Carabobo during the early national period were profound, first between landowners and their usually dark-skinned *jornaleros*, or tenants, and second between the landowners and the "national conservative oligarchy" and its allied business interests. For the *jornaleros* the repressive police regulations passed for the province of Carabobo in 1848 with respect to "day-workers and slaves" are a case in point. Both categories had to carry a sort of passport issued by their masters. A dayworker who left his employer "without a just cause," pretending to leave his debts behind, would be forced by the local judge to pay him double the amount (Materiales 1979, 168). In the early 1840s, boom conditions in Carabobo and Venezuela were replaced by lower prices on cocoa and coffee. At the same time, immigration, propounded as a remedy to the scarcity of labor, also dwindled. In 1841, the credit law of 1834 was made even more severe from the view of the indebted landowners, and the opposition to the government in Caracas grew. Thus, they were attracted to liberalism simply because that movement was anti-government. Thus it is no doubt more than a coincidence that the Liberals of Valencia would start the presidential election campaign in 1846, even though they could not agree on one candidate but split into three (González Guinan 1954, 4:118f.).[19] Meanwhile, the radical message of Antonio Leocadio Guzmán and his paper *El Venezolano* even reached the lower strata of the province. Two guerrilla chieftains, "Indian" Rangel and shopkeeper Ezequiel Zamora, started rebellions in Carabobo and adjoining provinces in September 1846.[20] In masses, slaves deserted their estates to join poor tenants and *jornaleros* in a fight for freedom and to kill the *godos*, the encompassing term for anybody more or less white, wealthy, and pro-Páez (Brito Figueroa 1975, 118ff.). The haciendas sacked were those of the *godos*, not those of their Liberal neighbors. But in early 1847, Rangel was cut down with a machete, and Zamora, like Guzmán, was taken prisoner. With the crucial support of Páez, José Tadeo Monagas now won the election campaign. A little later on, his break with the *godos* was provoked precisely by his commutation of the death sentences passed for the two radical leaders. Zamora was put in prison (from which he soon escaped), Guzmán sent into exile.

In 1848, the Carabobo provincial authorities decided to use the collective lands of the townships (*ejidos*) to distribute parcels of land to poor settlers. They would be granted ownership after ten years of cultivation. Unfortunately, however, as so often is true, the benevolent program seems to have had no effect whatsoever. According to the resolution, persons with criminal or rebel antecedents would not be able to enjoy this benefit. Because many, perhaps most, poor rural Carabobeños had taken part in the 1846–47 uprising, they were excluded (Matthews 1977, 29f.). Also, the National Law of 10 April 1848 on the distribution of the *baldíos* (as important in the Oriente) does not seem to have affected Carabobo to any notable degree.[21]

Although Carabobo did not escape being involved in the uprisings in 1853, it was not involved in the explicitly federal and official way that Cumaná was. Much more havoc was wreaked by the cholera epidemic of 1855. As many as 1,500 victims were reported from Valencia (González Guinan 1954, 5:295–305, 309f., 472–74).

In March 1858, the governor of Carabobo, Julián Castro, easily overthrew the discredited Monagas regime.[22] Characteristically, the Constitutional Assembly with its conservative majority met in Valencia some months later. However, in the Carabobo highlands guerrilla war under two peasant leaders soon set in. Their tenacious fight lasted until peace finally came five years later. By early 1860, most of Carabobo and more than half of its population were controlled by federal troops (Brito Figueroa 1975, 434).

As distinct from Cumaná, for example, Carabobo offers a picture of very intense sociopolitical struggle during the 1840s to 1860s. The blacks seem to have played a significant role both in 1846–47, the first *campesino* (peasant) war, as Brito Figueroa calls it, and after Abolition during the Federal War. It is quite possible that in Carabobo these struggles laid the basis for a rather fair rural structure, as symbolized by figure 1, however imaginative this painting may be.

The conflict between the *jornaleros* or tenants and the landlords had more important social results than that between the latter and the "national conservative oligarchy," which we have also tried to follow. Compared to Cumaná, for example, Carabobo was characterized by the fact that in 1961 no less than 93 percent of all privately owned arable land was cultivated by the owners (Vila 1966, 160). In Carabobo, federalism in the strict sense does not seem to have been at issue. Valencia could not possibly dream of challenging the supremacy of nearby Caracas.[23]

Barinas, Land of Cattle Thieves and Freedom Fighters

The city of Barinas, at the foot of the Andean mountain range, had been settled in the late sixteenth century, and cattle and horses were left to multiply in the immense plains of the llanos. The road from Barinas to Mérida and the Maracaibo lake, for long a kind of umbilical cord, remained horribly poor. To move northeast toward Valencia and Puerto Cabello was not easy either. There were many rivers to cross and it took a couple of weeks at least. A more natural though faraway

Figure 1. Venezuelan Landowner and His Wife, ca. 1850. Portrait of Miguel Alfonso Villasana and Gregoria Núñez Delgado de Villasana, attributed to the Maestro Zuloaga. *Source*: Galería de Arte Nacional, Caracas

outlet was to use the Apure and Orinoco rivers down to Angostura (renamed Ciudad Bolívar in 1846) in Guiana on the Atlantic.

Including parishes that later became parts of the province of Portuguesa, the province of Barinas had a total of 40,991 inhabitants in 1787 and 70,446 in 1810. By 1800 about 5,000 lived in the city, others in the small towns or on ranches in the countryside. Best known for its excellent tobacco, Barinas also contained fertile parts of land where cocoa (160 farms in 1787), indigo (39 farms), coffee, maíze, and other crops were grown.[24] The 2,124 African slaves kept in 1787 (5.2 percent of the population) were active in this sector. In 1810, their numbers had increased to 3,910 (5.6 percent). More important than agriculture, however, and on the increase was cattle wealth, even though cattle were even more numerous in the other llano province, Apure, to the south. Like cattle hands in other parts of the llanos, those of Barinas were heavily mulatto and zambo (*pardo*). In 1787, we know that Barinas cattle hands (llaneros) were employed by some 500 ranches (*hatos*) with more than 500,000 head of cattle and 100,000 horses (Tosta 1987, 425; McKinley 1985, 13, 119–21).

From the port of Nutrias on the Apure River, the main product of this resource, hides, were sent down to Guiana. Many testimonies make clear that this trade had a strong illegal flavor. Cattle and horse stealing (*abigeato*) was a deeply rooted practice in the llanos. The llaneros simply could not respect or even understand the notion of private property in the case of cattle.[25] In the 1830s, when authorities began to clamp down on the *abigeato*, general banditry was the Vaneros' response. In turn, bandits in times of political unrest turned into guerrilla warriors of whatever political cause. In any case, cattle wealth was subject to drastic oscillations over time. In Barinas-Apure (and part of Portuguesa), there were about 600,000 head of cattle and 200,000 horses in 1802. Estimates for 1832 drop down to about 170,000 and only 17,000, respectively. Horses were, of course, in extreme demand during the long period of wars, cattle almost as much. By 1839, cattle once again reached the half-million level (Tosta 1987, 247). Between 1839–40 and 1854–55, the export of hides quadrupled from 164,000 to 646,000 hides (Matthews 1977, 65).[26] Once again, the Federal War would greatly reduce the Barinas cattle wealth.

On the eve of Independence, a few aristocratic/merchant families, headed by the Marquess of Boconó and a total "elite" of about 1,000 people, shared the landed wealth and trade benefits of the city and province of Barinas (Tosta 1987, 47). The rest were petty traders, tenants, and cattle hands, like one José Antonio Páez, who was a peon of the landholder/politician Manuel Antonio Pulido. Under Tomás Boves, the mass of poor, dark-skinned llaneros fought in the name of the king against the white patriot elite, in Barinas as elsewhere in the llanos. Yáñez, a lieutenant of Boves, took the city of Barinas in 1812. The urban elite fled as well as it could along the mountain tracks and, ultimately, to New Granada. But Páez, precisely, by virtue of his tough charisma, was the man who would turn the wrath of the llaneros against the criollo royalists and Spaniards, the *godos* as they were called. Páez could hardly have guessed that less than thirty years later, a new llanero generation would see in him the very chief of the detested *godos*.

Peace returned to Barinas in 1819, with a population decimated by emigration and death. Agriculture had also suffered from the war but in peacetime too from the inroads of cattle and from the lack of farmhands. According to a British traveler in the 1830s, one tobacco harvest in Barinas was simply lost due to lack of workers (Hawkshaw

1975, 143). Most slaves had deserted or been drafted or killed. Only 1,200 were left (Lombardi 1971, 162). In 1830, after a decade of peace, the population of Barinas was only 94,000 (with another 20,000 in Apure; see table 1). Nine years later it had climbed to a total of 110,000. That year, according to geographer Agustín Codazzi, as many as 35 percent devoted themselves to cattle breeding, 45 percent to agriculture, and 25 percent to other industries and occupations. Codazzi describes in detail the malaria and other diseases which hampered population growth. Even though population had risen to 128,000 in 1843, two years later—in peacetime—mortality practically equalled nativity (Tosta 1987, 286).[27]

On the provincial level, the 1830s and early 1840s were a period of recovery and political stability in Barinas. On the grass-roots level, however, banditry thrived and the so-called Law of Flogging (*Ley de azotes* or *de hurtos*) of 1836, which sanctioned rough justice for *abigeato* and related crimes, seems merely to have increased social tensions in the countryside (Brito Figueroa 1966, 276f.).[28] At the same time, most ranch owners, indebted as they often were, were only slightly better off than their peons. From 1846 to 1848, the geographer Codazzi, politically conservative, was the governor of Barinas, for him a very unpleasant task, even though he gathered plentiful, valuable data on the province. By now, the party split in Barinas was a fact of life. Antonio Leocadio Guzmán's fellow Liberal journalist and demagogue in Barinas was Napoleón Sebastián Arteaga, an out-of-wedlock descendant of the last Marquess of Bocono. Arteaga's paper helped to spread liberalism in the urban sphere, at times in vitriolic terms. Codazzi, surprisingly in a Latin American context, accused the rural parish priests of having been especially active as liberal propagandists in the countryside. In Barinas in any case, the presidential elections of 1846 were easily won by Guzmán. Arteaga became Codazzi's successor. Under Arteaga education increased but so did corruption. In 1854 there was a minor uprising. Two years later Barinas was hit by cholera.

Really hard times came with the Federal War. In 1858, in the canton of Guanarito (Portuguesa), as told by historian Lisandro Alvarado (1956, 89–92), some salesmen who had been ruined in the indigo trade built up the so-called Indios de Guanarito faction. With slogans like "We are equal!," "Death to the Whites!," "Down with the Godos!," "Let's give the Indians a fatherland!," they succeeded in raising into rebellion both Indians of the communities (*resguardos*) and blacks who feared being enslaved once again.[29] Meanwhile, general Ezequiel Zamora, after opening the war in Coro, opted for descending to Barinas.

The city became his headquarters. To the extent possible in wartime, Zamora organized Barinas as a federal state. According to Brito Figueroa, he also organized a hard-core radical group of partisans within the federal army under his leadership (1975, 342). Reflecting French utopian ideas, Zamora in conversation with an English friend is said to have proclaimed: "Property is theft when it is not acquired through work." Thus, the property of a marquess was not sacred, while that of a small tobacco planter was (ibid., 346).

The image of Zamora as a fiery, visionary social revolutionary, painted by Brito Figueroa, is quietly but persuasively challenged by Adolfo Rodríguez, however. Far from promoting Abolition, as Brito claims (1975, 251), for instance, Zamora personally kept some slaves and *manumisos* until 1854, for whom in due course he received compensation (Rodríguez 1977, 199f.). Whatever the case, Zamora, a disciplinarian, did not like the brutal violence and outrages committed in the name of "federalism" by the irregular bands roaming the countryside such as the Indios de Guanarito, and he had a particularly bloodthirsty "general" shot. By the end of 1859, Zamora advanced against the central highlands and won the battle of Santa Inés. Shortly afterward, he himself was killed, in January 1860.

Now the war became even worse and less meaningful.[30] At the end of 1860, government forces occupied Barinas but for a short time only. Federalists in the llanos, like Arteaga, once again governor in 1862, were temporarily attracted to General Mósquera's Neo-Granadine Federation. After the Páez-Falcón agreement of Coche in 1863, which ended the war, the united llano state named Zamora (1861) once again was split into three: Barinas, Apure, and Portuguesa. In 1873, Barinas had 59,000 inhabitants. In nuclear districts like Barinas and Obispo, population actually declined, surely due to the protracted war (see table 2). Remarkably, population remained at that low level until 1936 (Vila 1963, 101).[31]

In Barinas in the nineteenth century, cities and some districts of agriculture appear like islands floating on the often stormy sea of the llanos. In the countryside there was in fact no law, nor execution of justice, merely violence as a consequence of the weakness of the social structure, the geographical isolation, and the vulnerable nature of external trade. Izard has claimed that the struggles of the llaneros and their chieftains were essentially of a defensive nature to free themselves from "Northern" exploitation. He does not pin down such causality convincingly, however. While liberalism meant something in the cities of Barinas, federalism was only an empty slogan for everybody, with the possible exception of Ezequiel Zamora. Though most llaneros were neither purely Indian nor black but racially mixed, their hatred for any white taken for a *godo* is amply demonstrated in the records.[32]

Let me return to the questions raised in the first part of this chapter, questions to be tested against our three regional cases. What was the power of the national state on that level? What was the relationship between the elites and the masses? How did the masses react to what followed upon the socioracial discrimination of the colonial period?

The region of Cumaná was characterized by stable *caudillo* rule. It was the cradle of federalism and, together with the rest of the Oriente, exercised considerable influence on national affairs during the Monagas period. Social tensions appear to have been relatively weak.

Carabobo was close to the seat of the central government and normally submitted to its will. At certain moments, however, Valencia assumed a role of national importance. The socioracial struggle in Carabobo was intense, especially due to the great importance of slave labor.

The socioracial struggle was also intense in Barinas, a distant region but clearly of basic strategic importance during the civil wars because of its location and wealth in terms of livestock, horses, and tough warriors. Here, the traditional elite was crushed step by step. In the countryside, social structure was much more loose than in the coastal provinces. In Barinas, the colonial patterns of socioracial discrimination had never been deeply rooted. In the course of various outbursts of violence, culminating during the Federal War, there emerged in the llanos a kind of equality of the poor, of whatever color they might be.

CHAPTER 5

The Masses Face the Modernizing Ambitions of the National State

The Background of the Quebra Quilos Movement in Imperial Brazil

FROM THE mid-nineteenth century until the 1880s, no state in Latin America could compete with the centralized Brazilian Empire in terms of national cohesion and political stability.[1] In the person of Emperor Pedro II, constitutionally endowed with a wide-ranging "Poder Moderador," imperial Brazil enjoyed a degree of legitimacy unknown in any Spanish American republic.

According to conventional wisdom, the Empire was merely a tool used by the large plantation owners to promote their interests. Recently this view has been strongly challenged, however. The successful war against Paraguay, 1865–70, and the "modernization" and expansion of the armed forces which it brought with it, certainly gave the state a greater potential. Especially from 1868 onward, the national elite was composed mainly of lawyers and judges with the law degree of *bacharel* while the members or dependents of the old plantocracy saw their share decline.[2] Moreover, historian Steven Topic (1985) has shown that the rather modest resources that the central administration was able to distribute did not benefit export interests unduly but rather internal development. "Modernization" of a West European type clearly stood high on the imperial agenda. The British influence was no doubt particularly great and has also been the object of research. Here, however, I will examine a most un-English modernizing feature—that is, the introduction of the metric system.

The timing in Brazil was surprisingly early. It was the new liberal government of the Marquess of Olinda that issued the imperial decree of 26 June 1862, introducing the "French" system.[3] A period of ten years was reserved for the process of application. (After a difficult period of introduction, 1789–99, France itself sanctioned the metric system without reservations only in 1837. Germany would not adopt the system until 1868, when it replaced no less than 3,000 different measures and weights.) However, we may suppose that little happened with the metric system in Brazil after 1862 until another government, a conservative one, took up the question in 1872. On 28 June 1871, in the emperor's absence, the president of the Council of State, Viscount Rio Branco, forced through the Law of Free Birth (*Lei do Ventre livre*), which foredoomed black slavery.[4] Rio Branco, trained in mathematics, also saw to it that instructions concerning the application of the 1862 decree on the metric system were issued on 18 September 1872. Severe punishment (jail or high fines) would be meted out for infractions from 1 July 1873 onward.

To carry out such a measure so quickly in an enormous country like Brazil with its extremely poor communications was well-nigh impossible. The popular cry that one should smash the new scales (*Quebra os quilos!*) was first heard in the course of a street tumult in Rio de Janeiro in 1871. As everywhere, an innovation like this was likely to run into opposition, at least among more popular strata, who were familiar with traditional measures, however irrational they appeared. People were afraid, and probably rightly so, that any new measure imposed from above would be used to cheat them.[5] But in the capital, of course, real resistance was out of question.

Instead, such resistance began in the interior of the Northeast, where application had been postponed until mid-1874. In the provinces of Paraíba and Pernambuco, in particular, the Quebra Quilos movement became widespread and popular. It has been studied in an intelligent article by the Canadian historian Roderick J. Barman (1977) and in a book by a Brazilian student, Armando Souto Maior (1978), most unsystematic and barely analytical but full of interesting data. An article by Geraldo Irenéo Joffily (1976) has also provided valuable information. The book by Linda Lewin on family politics in Paraíba (1987) is devoted to the "Old Republic" from 1889 onward; her introductory account is invaluable for our subject here. These works mentioned have been my main sources. Yet even for a mere description of the riots—a total of about a hundred riots took place between late November 1874 and January 1875—a broader framework is required.

First, a Law of Military Enlistment was issued on 26 September 1874, with the explicit purpose of making military recruitment somewhat less harsh and arbitrary than it had been so far. Still, students and wealthy people continued to escape from service. Whatever the good intentions of the authorities, the Enlistment law, the census held in

1872, and the national registration of slaves could all give the impression of being links in the chain of an even worse exploitation of the peasants of the interior, free as they were at the time but poor and of dark skin, like the slaves.

Second, and probably no less important, the traditionally uneventful and smooth relationship between state and church in Brazil became highly strained from 1872 onward. Behind this was the ultramontane wave set in motion by Pope Pius IX. His violent condemnation of freemasonry in the encyclical Quanta Cura of 1864 had never received due approval (*exequatur*) by Pedro II, a convinced regalist, and thus had never been communicated to the Brazilian clergy (Mecham 1966, 271). Therefore, when the new and ardent bishop of Olinda suddenly applied the encyclical in Recife, expelling all masons from the religious brotherhoods (*irmandades*), he simply committed a crime according to state norms. Masonry of a usually very bland and non-anticlerical type was enormously widespread among the upper and middle strata of Brazil. Numerous priests were members. Rio Branco himself was a grand master. In November 1873, the bishop of Olinda and his colleague in Pará were arrested and put on trial. By June 1874, they had both been sentenced to four years in prison (the emperor saving them from the additional "hard labor"). Their crime was that of having sought to "impede the will of the executive and moderative power." Eventually, skillful negotiations between the Empire and the Vatican brought about a face-saving compromise. Yet in late 1874, the situation was still very tense (Mecham 1966, 273). In the backlands of the Northeast, the propagation of the Catholic Revival by Capuchins and Italian Jesuits who roamed around there could not but raise suspicions on the part of the authorities. As soon as he heard about the Quebra Quilos unrest in Paraíba, Rio Branco, on 25 November 1874, wrote to the emperor that one of these preachers, the remarkable Father José Maria de Ibiapina, "appears to be the agitator. . . . The pretext is the recruitment, the new weights and measures, and the Religious Question" (Souto Maior 1978, 65).

Still, Rio Branco does not mention a fourth factor that was not the least important one: the introduction of new municipal taxes in Paraíba in August–October 1874. Proposed by the various municipal *câmaras*, they were approved, one after another, by the Provincial Assembly (Quebra-Kilos 1937, 153–57). Tax farmers were in charge of collecting these taxes on the weekly markets of the various towns. The so-called *imposto de chão* was imposed on every load of grain or vegetables sold in markets. It was the refusal of the peasants to pay this tax at

Map 6. Northeast Brazil and the Quebra Quilo Uprising.
Source: Barman 1977, 406

the weekly village market on 31 October 1874 in Fagundes, near Campina-Grande in the interior of Paraíba, that actually triggered the first riot.

These scenes must also be seen within a wider socioeconomic and regional framework. Most of the riots took place in the transitional zones called Agreste and Brejos, situated between the forested Zona da Mata along the coast with all the sugar plantations, and the semiarid Sertão, where cattle breeding was the main way of eking out a meager and precarious livelihood (see map 6). The Brejos are higher, cooler, somewhat humid areas, almost oases where even sugar may be grown. They are situated on the eastern slopes of the Borburema mountain range, stretching from Rio Grande do Norte to Alagoas in the South with an average altitude of some 600 meters. The Agreste mixes *caatinga* (dry shrub) with quite fertile land. It receives 1,200 millimeters of rainfall yearly at the most and has thin soils (Webb 1974, 12 and passim; Lewin 1987, 47–50). Prior to the nineteenth century, most of the Agreste (like the Sertão) had been fit only for ranching. Cattle fairs gave rise to towns like Campina Grande and Areia in Paraíba, and Caruarú in Pernambuco. Campina Grande, founded in 1790, had some 4,000 inhabitants in 1864. Areia, situated in a Brejos area, had become a city in 1846. Its cattle fair was reputed to be the largest one in Paraíba. In the nineteenth century, herbaceous cotton became the main product of the Brejos and Agreste while tree-cotton was planted on very circumscribed plots of land in the Sertão. Farming techniques in any case were primitive.[6]

With respect to human conditions, the ecological and economic division was more important than the administrative division between the Alagoas, Pernambuco, Paraíba, and Rio Grande do Norte provinces.[7] Cotton, the major part of which was exported via Recife, Pernambuco, was grown by peasants on rather small parcels of land. Very little is known for sure about land tenure, at least prior to the census of 1920. That is why recent students like Barman and Lewin differ widely in their characterizations of the pattern existing during the late nineteenth century. Barman underscores the de facto control of the land by the peasants who used it, even though "on paper" it belonged to some large estate with a landlord mainly interested in cattle breeding. By the 1870s slaves were also quite few in this transition zone (5–7 percent, according to Barman). Apart from cotton for sale, the peasants also grew manioc, beans, and maíze for their own subsistence. They were sturdy and independent, even though they were integrated with credit networks extending from Recife and local urban merchants (Barman 1977, 408–10). Lewin, on the other hand, stresses the threatening impact of the cotton advance on rural society after the mid-nineteenth century in the interior of Paraíba, her field of study. Unclaimed arable land was no longer available. And the landlords did maintain effective control over their tenant clients, that is, the vast majority of the "peasants." Local boss rule, *coronelismo*, reflected the pattern of land tenure, even though latifundia were few or nonexistent (Lewin 1987, 70–73).

Ever since the early colonization, the provinces of Alagoas, Pernambuco, and Rio Grande do Norte had relied almost exclusively on the sugar exports from the plantations on the coast. In the latter part of the nineteenth century, the decline of sugar exports became clear to everybody, however. The plantations sold a large part of their slaves, too expensive to keep, to coffee plantations further south which could better afford them. Free tenants (*moradores*) took their places. At the same time, however, cotton experienced a rising demand on the world market, particularly so during the "cotton famine" caused by the U.S. Civil War, and cotton was a "poor man's crop" which was above all produced in the Agreste and Brejos zones. Admittedly, in the Sertão also, there were small moist areas such as floodplains where cultivation could be pursued. Here cotton-trees had been introduced around 1800. Most of that cotton was hauled over some 600 kilometers of land to be shipped overseas from Recife, like the produce of the Agreste and Brejos zones (Webb 1974, 115ff.).

As a result of these economic changes, the demographic pattern also changed significantly. In 1782, Paraíba was estimated to have some 52,000 to 53,000 inhabitants, 64 percent of whom settled on the coast, 28 percent in the Sertão, and only 8 percent in the Brejos-Agreste zones. In 1872, the census revealed rapid population growth, to 375,000, no less. But now only 25 percent remained on the coast, while the Brejos-Agreste zones housed 31 percent and the distant Sertão 44 percent (Lewin 1987, 64). In 1869–71 the production of cotton in Paraíba rapidly dropped. The harvest of 1871–72 represented a recovery, but the next year saw a new drop (see graph 1).

Export figures from Recife, Pernambuco, which should include most of the Paraíba cotton, give a similar but not identical picture. For the period 1869–74, the nadir of cotton exports was reached in 1873/74. Even more relevant from a social point of view were the price trends in cotton. They were declining considerably from the end of the Civil War onward. The year 1870–71 was an especially bad year. In 1874, according to Barman, the fall of cotton prices put the Agreste producers under heavy pressure. Linked to the world depression of 1873 as it was, the export market of the Northeast now "collapsed" (Barman 1977, 414).[8]

Before discussing the Quebra Quilos riots, it is, however, also worthwhile to consider a very significant antecedent studied by Geraldo I. Joffily. This was a popular movement in the very same area of Paraíba triggered by the imperial decision of 18 June 1851 to have the

Kilograms

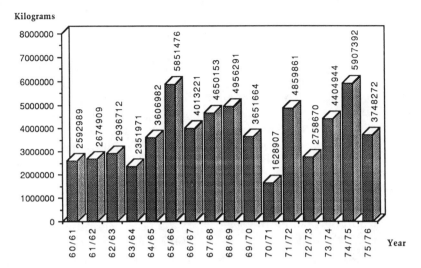

Graph 1. Cotton Production in Paraíba, 1860/61–1875/76.
Source: Lewin 1987, 68

registry of baptisms and funerals transferred from parish priests to civil public servants. Some riots took place, apparently due to the obligation to assign the slave or free status of individuals, always a delicate matter. Provincial authorities from the president downward took it calmly, however, and peace was restored even before the application of the law had been postponed (in fact until 1889) in January 1852 (Joffily 1976, 77–83).[9] Perhaps it was the suspicion of the authorities in 1874–75 that the church was involved which made them so much more nervous than they had been in 1851–52.

The Riots

The Quebra Quilos riots took many forms.[10] Let me take a rather large-scale example, that of the town of Caruarú, in the province of Pernambuco, where on 12 December 1874, at 10 A.M., some 400 people from outside entered the marketplace, armed with knives and blunderbusses (*bocamartes*). Joined by most marketgoers, they cheered liberty, religion, and the authorities. But they also cried that they wanted the abolition of the taxes and the metric system and that they would struggle until death for that goal. Some of them then entered the town hall, burned its archives, and destroyed the new standards of weights and measures kept there. Toward 4 P.M., all those who had come to the town six hours earlier withdrew but threatened to come back if new attempts were made to collect the new taxes.

Most riots were on a much smaller scale, however. Some, perhaps most, rioters were unarmed.[11] In any case the smashing of the metric standards seems to have constituted a ritual act that bound the widespread, disparate movement together somehow and also gave it its name. The most remarkable feature of the riots, however, is that the rioters very seldom hurt or killed anyone, at least unless attacked by "friends of order."[12] Landowners and local officials also usually remained passive observers, whatever their thoughts or feelings. Landowners had no sympathy for the metric system or the new taxes either, but, of course, they did not like to see their titles burn. At times, they succeeded in persuading the *matutos*—as the peasants of the Agreste were called—not to destroy the records of the public notaries. This was the only major point on which their interests differed from those of the peasants. The judicial accounts taken after the suppression of the movement are full of names of military titleholders, even in the most outlying areas. These were militia officers, often landowners, of the Guarda Nacional and just as passive as the rest of the landowners, the district judges, and the police chiefs.[13] At least once, however, we meet a couple of landowners who brought their own workers to fight the Quebra Quilos, causing some bloodshed (Souto Maior 1978, 179).

The general pattern of the outbreaks seems to be that they spread with a surprisingly great speed within a wide geographical space. First, they started at some smaller marketplace (like Fagundes) and then exploded in the nearest larger one (like Campina Grande). Second, they spread generally southward from Paraíba to Pernambuco and, to a lesser extent, Alagoas. They seldom entered the Zona da Mata. Souto Maior has also found outbreaks of a similar kind in Ceará to the Northwest but during the latter part of 1875. These, however, were protests directed solely against the Law of Enlistment and with women as main actors (Souto Maior 1978, 188f.).

On the whole, calm followed every riot; people just returned to their everyday toil. Above the village or town level, no leaders can be discerned. Troops from Rio de Janeiro, however, were on their way. In late November, an infantry batallion and artillery were sent to Paraíba. These troops arrived in the city of Parahyba (now called João Pessoa) on 7 December under the orders of Colonel Severiano Martins Da Fonseca (a brother of the marshal and future president of Brazil). His orders were to "ensure the introduction of the metric system, to seize the rebels, and to guarantee the constituted authorities, even those re-

placed by the people invading the cities and towns of central [Paraíba]"
(Quebra-Kilos 1937, 101f.). On Christmas Eve, the troops entered
Campina Grande. Many prisoners were taken and cruelly put to
death.[14] Others were forced to join the army, something which in Latin
America is usually seen as a severe punishment. On the national level,
however, from the very beginning, ultramontane priests, above all
those of foreign origin, were seen as the main culprits. A few Jesuits
who had only returned to the Northeast in 1866, after Pombal's expulsion in 1759, were simply put on board a Europe-bound ship and
sent back. Among the Quebra Quilos "leaders" detained and sent to
Rio de Janeiro were a couple of parish priests.

On 17 September 1875, when the emperor granted amnesty to the
recalcitrant bishops and their partisans, however, the Quebra Quilos
leaders were also included (Joffily 1976, 127). The image of the Quebra
Quilos as a fanatic, reactionary rabble, paradoxically enough, was
above all presented in conservative papers. Liberal papers, on the other
hand, who did not have to support the imperial government, tended
to take a more understanding view. A professor at the prestigious Law
School of Pernambuco wrote in a liberal paper an account of the Quebra Quilos movement on 1 December 1874:

> The people are a constant victim of barbarous military recruit-
> ment, a real man hunt. Also, they are squeezed by excessive taxes,
> agreed upon without any reservations, by unanimous Chambers;
> the people are starving and naked though born in a most fertile
> country [!]; commerce and agriculture are in a more deplorable
> state than ever. . . . On the top of everything else, there is this fatal
> religious question, the general anxiety of conscience. Such are the
> causes of this deplorable sedition. (Souto Maior 1978, 57f.)[15]

Interestingly enough, the same Colonel Da Fonseca, some months
later, reached a rather similar conclusion. In March 1875 he reported
to the minister of war that in January he sent a circular letter to the
various district judges requesting information on the extent and forms
of the outbreaks. On the basis of such material received, Da Fonseca
claimed that the riots had three causes: (1) poverty and heavy taxation,
(2) the ignorance of, in particular, the population of the backlands, and
(3) the demoralization of authority for lack of support and means of
repression which actually meant a "protection of crime." Behind the
movement, though, he discerned "two powerful enemies": first, "fanaticism," that is, the religious, and second, the intrigues of malcon-
tented politicians. The colonel emphasizes, in fact, the unfairness of
the taxation passed by the Provincial Assembly and the cynical behavior

of the tax farmers when trying to collect such taxes. Da Fonseca also blames the merchants and landowners who remained "neutral" or indifferent to the riots because they, too, detested the taxes and had at home attacked them fiercely (Quebra-Kilos 1937, 118–20).

On the national level, the Quebra Quilos were soon forgotten. The Rio Branco government, the longest lasting one of the imperial era, fell in June 1875, due mainly to financial problems, in particular connected with the collapse of the important Banco Mauá.[16]

On the northeastern regional level, the movement's traces would soon be overshadowed by a much more traumatic experience, the dreadful drought of 1877–79, which caused mass starvation in the Sertão and the exodus in all directions of the survivors. Later, in 1893, in the distant northwestern corner of Bahía, a part of the Sertão, the charismatic lay preacher António Conselheiro would establish the holy City of Canudos, which it would take several, increasingly massive and sanguinary military campaigns to destroy, this tragedy immortalized by Euclides da Cunha and also the subject of a recent novel by Peruvian author Mario Vargas Llosa. In this same arid and distant area, in southernmost Ceará, another charismatic religious leader, "Father Cícero," would build a stronghold in Joaseiro. In the same central part of the Sertão, in the early twentieth century, social banditry would reach its culmination with the famous Lampião, killed in 1938.[17]

A Critical Analysis of the Movement

The Quebra Quilos movement has to be placed within a continuum of regional social protest. In order to elaborate its profile better, however, let us check it against a general analytical scheme of rural mass movements.

First, what structural factors can be discerned behind the emergence of the movement? I believe they were partly economic, such as the striking vulnerability of cotton exports. But they were surely also social, connected with a worsening of tenancy conditions, as I shall soon discuss. There was also the fear that military recruitment would become an even worse plague than it already was. Furthermore, the preaching of ultramontane priests, whether itinerant missionaries or some of the curates, clearly undermined the legitimate authority of officeholders from district judges upward; they were suspected of being masons whether they were so or not. Apart from cotton exports and tenancy conditions, these factors were not specific to the northeastern provinces only. They were clearly all at work there, however.[18]

Second, what factors actually triggered the movement? Here, I think, the *imposto do chão,* in the towns of Paraíba at least, and the imposition of the new measures and weights combined to produce an explosive situation on the village or small market town level. As Robert Levine put it (1988, 562), the innovation "threatened the informal mechanisms of the *feira* market system."

Third, what was the ethnic or social composition of the movement? It appears as if the crowds comprised almost the whole range of local social strata, the *matutos,* hardly a very stratified society. Most were dark-skinned but, characteristically for Brazil, *brancos do algodão* ("cotton whites") was what they were often called, regardless of phenotype (Andrade 1963, 91). The upper stratum, the landowners, appear to have played a mediatory or, as Da Fonseca suspected, an ambivalent role. However, there is interesting information that in Campina Grande, for example, a couple of weeks after the first Quebra Quilos riots, the slaves used the opportunity to demand their liberty from terrified slave owners (Quebra-Kilos 1937, 109, 115f.).

The question of leadership is also highly relevant. Despite all the suspicions of the contemporaries, no leaders of the Quebra Quilos, at least above the grass-roots level, can be discerned. This is a striking contrast to, for example, the Canudos and Joaseiro phenomena.

How was the movement organized? Being leaderless, the Quebra Quilos could hardly be organized in any strict sense, and the various outbursts were not identical.[19] Yet, its rapid spread suggests a probably completely informal but still efficient information network of a type sometimes to be found in illiterate, poor societies. Did peddlers possibly play an important role?

To what extent did the adversary help to escalate the conflict? As the Guarda Nacional does not seem to have acted as such, regular troops were naturally rather slow in arriving. By then, the riots had already subsided so that merely repression, not escalation, would eventually take place. Da Fonseca's and his subordinates' reports show this very clearly. At most, there was some exchange of fire with "rebels" in the woods. This naturally raises the question of whether the military intervention was needed at all. In the Chamber of Deputies in Rio de Janeiro in 1879, a Liberal politician from Paraíba simply put the blame on the Conservative president of the province who, for reasons of his own, opted for the use of violence (instead of smoother methods, as did his predecessor in 1852; Joffily 1976, 124f.).

What was the area finally controlled by the movement? In this case, territorial control is not an appropriate term, in contrast to, for example, Canudos. But the outer limits reached seem rather clear, from Barman's map. The Quebec Quilos did not cross the São Francisco

River in the south. In the north, the movement in Rio Grande do Norte seems to have had a different character. Market networks appear to have been at work in the spread.[20]

What was the duration of the movement? In general terms, less than two months. On the community level usually much less, perhaps only a few hours. At times, however, new riots would eventually take place. Very short duration is, of course, what could be expected from a movement with no general leadership and with an extremely low organizational level. This is a type of *jacquerie*, to use a term from French medieval history.[21]

Were there any potential or actual allies of the movement? As potential allies, some of the landowners but not all and certainly not the sugar *fazendeiros* of the Zona da Mata would qualify. The ultramontane Catholic religious must have enjoyed the popular condemnations of the masons, but otherwise they kept their fingers off the pie. Would the provincial liberal parties have considered the use of the Quebra Quilos for purposes of their own? Probably only as an argument for their anticonservative propaganda.[22]

What were the values of the participants? The mentalités of the rugged inhabitants of the Sertão have often been described, by Euclides Da Cunha and others. The *matutos*, after all, were settlers who led a somewhat less rough and hazardous life than the *sertanejos*. At the same time, they had a more independent life style than the coastal *moradores* and other dependents of the plantations. What seems to be relevant here must be their piety within the frame of popular religion and their naive faith in the emperor as a distant, almost mythological father figure. The Quebra Quilos did not blame him, he had just been deceived by godless masons (Souto Maior 1978, 58).[23] Also, the *matutos* believed that regardless of land titles, the crops they grew should not be appropriated by others. As one of them told the court, "The fruit of the soil (*o chão*) belongs to the people and tax ought not to be paid on it" (Barman 1977, 409).

Normally it is important to determine what were the goals of the leaders of a rural mass movement, in the view of its foes and as shown by the events. With no leaders in the case of the Quebra Quilos, however, there would be no authoritative statements about goals. As to the foes, they have little to say of substance on this point. The events, to the degree that we know them, therefore constitute our only worthwhile source. It then appears quite clear that the aim was to prevent the new taxation at a moment of great economic uncertainty, to impede the new weights and measures, and to impede the new, possibly worse form of military recruitment. The return of the Quebra Quilos to everyday life as soon as they had made their action also strongly suggests that at least for the time being they had no other conscious goals.

Finally, did the movement have any results in the short or long run? While Souto Maior considers the Quebra Quilos movement to be just another tragedy in the somber past of the northeastern backlands, Barman argues that the movement was successful, as seen in relation to its goals.[24] He has found that military enlistment under the new rules failed and was abandoned in the region. Further, no new census was taken in 1880 as the law required. Finally, the attempts at introducing the metric system in the interior were abandoned. As Barman puts it, all this meant the end of the imperial government's so-called crusade for moral and material development. "While not the sole reason . . . the Quebra Quilo revolt was certainly the immediate cause" (422). For all of Barman's expertise, however, I feel that he awards the movement an excessively important role. Once what the authorities believed to be a danger had passed, it was quite natural for them to relapse into passivity. The momentum of the Rio Branco government was probably broken anyway, regardless of what the miserable peasants in the backlands of the Northeast would or would not do.

Moreover, Lewin in her book on family politics in Paraíba (1987), contrary to Barman but without discussing his thesis, emphasizes the political failure of the Quebra Quilos rebels. They were unable to prevent "the aggressive regulation of weekly markets by the government, which included the implementation of more determined efforts to collect taxes." Also, the "singular brutality" of the military repression "offered a powerful object lesson to future peasant rebels" (75). More importantly, Lewin places the rebellion in connection with the imposition of the so-called *sujeição* labor system. This important institution (not even mentioned by Barman) meant that the rural tenants of the Northeast, although legally free, had to perform increasingly onerous labor for their landlords. Some small freeholders became tenants who were subjected to the *sujeição*. In the northeastern backlands of the 1870s, peasants were squeezed between falling earnings from cotton sales and high prices on what they had to buy. They found it more difficult to pay their debts to their landlords and others and consequently lost their credit. According to Lewin, the imposition of *sujeição* labor coincided with the Quebra Quilos revolt. First, this would make the efforts of the landlords to impose the new labor system a mighty structural cause of the revolt. Second, the suppression of the revolt ought to have implied the weakening or even elimination of any further peasant resistance against the *sujeição*. Clearly, research in primary sources would be needed to reach more firm conclusions about the relationship between this system and the revolt. Yet Lewin's interpretation (74–76) seems to me much more probable than Barman's. It fits much better with the long-term "development of the underdevelopment" of the Northeast.[25] In any case, the questions we have raised lead us to some final reflections on the relationship between the state (the Empire of Brazil as it was) and the rural masses of the northeastern backlands.

At the time, Brazil had built up a relatively huge central bureaucratic apparatus of government. It was trying to extend that apparatus to the provinces of the periphery. The presidents of the provinces were appointed by the emperor and were often changed from one province to another in order to make them serve the interests of the center rather than those of a particular province. President Lucena in Pernambuco, for example, served there from late 1872 until May 1875, his colleague Da Cunha in Paraíba from late 1873 until March 1876. From 1846 onward, municipal judges and police chiefs were also appointed by central authorities. Historian Fernando Uricoechea, who discusses imperial state-building in Brazil in Weberian terms, finds the foundation of the Empire to be "patrimonial." He also states that top-level decision making was usually arrived at through compromises with regional elites and family networks. Moreover, he finds the Guarda Nacional, built up during the unstable 1830–40s, to be a mainly patrimonial creation. Interestingly enough, however, Uricoechea dates the decay of the Guarda Nacional from an imperial decree in 1873 which curtailed the Guard's functions in favor of the police force.[26] This does suggest that part of the explanation why the local order in the northeastern interior broke down so easily in face of the Quebra Quilos had something to do with this crucial transition from one type of security system to another, or, to use Uricoechea and Weber's, from patrimonial to bureaucratic domination. As the former puts it, the Quebra Quilos movement was no mere episode of religious fanaticism but a "conscious but intuitive and ineffable protest against bourgeois rationality, against the abstract notion of rational calculus that was subjecting the whole society to a unified system of laws" (1980, 157). The Quebra Quilos were the "Luddites" of the backlands.

Using Michael Mann's perspective instead, one can hardly find a more typical ingredient of infrastructural power than the territorial extension and imposition of a unified system of weights and measures (1984, 192). Yet, the imperial attempt to impose such a system and the other innovations we have been discussing was pathetically premature.[27] In northeastern Brazil, the provincial presidents and provincial elites centered on the coast exercised no effective control over the

Agreste area and its *matuto* settlers. The military intervention and the ensuing repression came too late to be considered "rational." It was rather, through its arbitrary brutality, a display of traditional, despotic power. Thus, if anything, the Quebra Quilos revolt helped to reveal the crucial weaknesses behind the proud imperial façade.[28]

CHAPTER 6

The Native-born Face the Promotion of Immigration by the State

Argentina: A Country Transformed by Immigration

FEW COUNTRIES in the world have experienced such a drastic transformation in demographic and social terms as Argentina did. Between 1871 and 1914, some 5.9 million immigrants poured into a country which in the former year had fewer than 2 million inhabitants. To be sure, return migration was also very high and only 3.1 million opted for settling down. Yet in 1895, foreigners totalled a fourth of Argentina's 4 million population. In 1914, they formed as much as 30 percent of the 7.9 million total population. In 1930, about 23 percent were still classified as foreigners (Cornblit 1967, 222). Even more significant, the immigrants, as they tend to do, formed a considerably larger share of the economically active population than of the total one. In 1895, their share of that population was 39 percent; in 1914, 46 percent (Germani 1968, 283).

Out of the total flow, no less than 80 percent came from Italy and Spain, and a large part of the remainder came from Central and Eastern Europe. These were all areas severely hit by the agricultural depression of the 1880s, which in turn was largely caused by the imports of grains produced by other European migrants in the Midwest of the United States. The curve of Argentine immigration underwent great variations over time (as shown by graph 2).

From 1876 to 1890, the rise was really impressive. With the financial and political crisis in 1890, it fell to a much lower level. It should be noted, of course, that after the abolition of slavery in 1888, southern Brazil was able to present an attractive alternative, especially for Italian emigrants. Argentine gross immigration increased from the later 1890s onward, culminating in 1912 (379,117 immigrants).[1] The two censuses of 1895 and 1914, which constitute our main sources for the

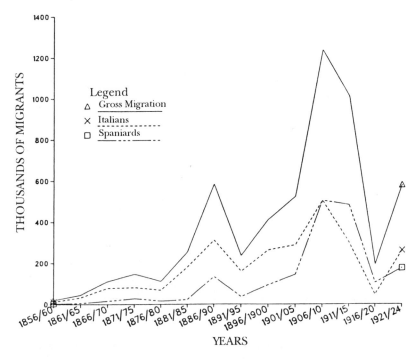

Graph 2. Gross Migration to Argentina and the Number of Italians and Spanish, 1856/60–1921/24.
Source: Mörner 1985, 54

impact of immigration, took place during descending phases of the curve. In fact, immigration was drastically reduced during World War I. During the 1920s the curve once again arced, but to a lower extent than before, that was leveled by the Depression.

Naturally, the migratory phenomenon had deep economic and social implications. In fact, the positive correlation between the exports of wheat and flour and gross immigration for 1871–1911 is strikingly high ($r = 0.8072$; $r^2 = 0.6516$; see graph 3).

Moreover, the importance of European immigrants within certain socioeconomic sectors was even greater than general immigration figures would suggest. In 1895, for example, 81 percent of the owners of industrial enterprises and 74 percent of the owners of business firms were foreigners. About 60 percent of blue-collar workers and other industrial employees were foreigners. In 1914 that last share had fallen to 50 percent, but meanwhile industrial employment had swollen from

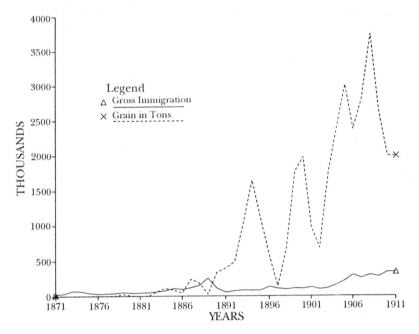

Graph 3. Export of Wheat and Flour from Argentina and Gross Immigration, 1871–1910 (r(corr.) = .8072; r^2 = .6516).
Source: Mörner 1985, 64

176,000 to 410,000 jobs (Cornblit 1967, 229). Also, in 1914, the share of foreign industrial proprietors had sunk to 66 percent. This may have been mainly due to generational succession. For foreign-owned business firms, the share remained the same. According to Oscar Cornblit (1967, 227), within Argentine industry, "foreigners tended to be associated with the more modern establishments while the native-born" largely controlled more traditional branches. Politically, however, the Union of Industrialists (UIA) yielded little influence because most members were unnaturalized foreigners (Solberg 1970, 273).

In 1895, 52 percent of the native-born adults were illiterate, whereas only 35 percent of the immigrants were. The immigrant 35 percent illiteracy rate persisted until 1914, however, when that for the native-born had been reduced to 39 percent.

Although difficult to pin down in figures, it is quite clear that the emerging labor unions and above all their leadership and militants held an even larger share of foreigners than their share of the industrial labor force. This was true both of Anarchists and Socialists, who competed for the allegiance of labor. Thus, at both ends of the industrial spectrum, the presence of the foreigners was very striking indeed. On the other hand, even in 1914 the native-born overwhelmingly controlled the ownership of land, Argentina's traditional resource of both power and wealth. While foreigners, to a greater or lesser degree from region to region, had become numerous among the middle rural strata, it appears that, with some regional exceptions, simple rural workers were mainly recruited among the native-born. In some areas, they were recruited from neighboring countries: a total of 11.5 percent of all immigrants in 1895, 8.6 percent in 1914.

Thus, European mass immigration had set the scene for considerable imbalances and tensions. For the native-born, the "gringos," as all of the Europeans were termed, appeared as simultaneously enviable and ridiculous creatures. Their direct political role would be much more modest than their role in society and economy.

Immigration Policies Pursued by the State and the Political Parties

Until the 1870s, Argentina was dominated in every sense by a ranching oligarchy linked to pastoral exports. However, a handful of European immigrants induced to settle down in the province of Santa Fé from the 1850s onward survived all kinds of hardships to become the pioneers in growing wheat. Toward the late 1880s, wheat growers had become massive exporters of grains for the international market. In turn, this led more enlightened landlords and thus the national government to earnestly favor mass immigration, as the wheat economy naturally was much more labor-intensive than the pastoral economy had ever been. In 1888 the national government even began to subsidize immigrant passages. In the course of two years, a third of all immigrants had been subsidized in this way (125,000 individuals). The severe financial crisis of 1890 soon forced the Argentine government to suspend this practice, however. In any case, the fares continued to be low. Around 1900, an agricultural laborer could be reimbursed for the cost of the voyage to Argentina with just two weeks' work. This fact gave rise to a transatlantic seasonal labor movement. The so-called *golondrinas* (swallows) spent only harvest time (that is, around October–May) in the South, the rest in their Mediterranean homeland with its inverse harvest season. Only in permanently settling down in Argentina did the *golondrinas* become immigrants in any real sense.

The general return-migration rate was very high, 47 percent for

Argentina, from 1847 to 1924 (Mörner 1985, 50). Migrants returned either because they originally intended to do so once they had earned enough money or because they were disappointed. A large factor behind this latter type of return migration was the difficulty of buying land. For several reasons, the frequency of return migration also varied widely between various national groups. During the period 1857–1924, among the two principal groups, the Italians had a 50 percent return rate and the Spaniards a 43 percent one. Return migration also underwent drastic oscillations over time. During the first years following the crisis of 1890, emigration exceeded immigration. Another dip after 1910 worried authorities. Thus, in 1911 the Argentine government forced the shipping companies to double the price of passages to Europe (Mörner 1985, 69).

The elite believed that immigration should achieve economic expansion without altering the country's sociopolitical status quo. Immigrants who were really successful, however, were likely to raise suspicion, fear, and envy among lower-class native-born. In Argentina, "Turkish" and Jewish groups were especially defamed. In 1919, a pogrom took place in Buenos Aires, as is described below.

The defense of the sociopolitical status quo became even more explicit with respect to immigrant activity within the working class, such as anarchists and union organizers. With the purpose of denying such elements entrance or assuring their expulsion, the Conservative government promulgated the so-called Laws of Residency in 1902 and the Law of Social Defense in 1910. Thus, as underlined by historian Carl Solberg, Argentina's traditionally very pro-immigration, liberal policy, expressed above all in the 1853 Constitution, was substantially modified.

While immigrants were most busy in promoting their common interests by forming associations of various kinds and building up unionism, they lacked interest in becoming citizens through naturalization. After all, the Constitution made it very clear that aliens should "enjoy . . . all of the civil rights of the citizen" in the economic sense, freely practice their religion, and so forth. They were not "obliged to assume citizenship, nor to pay forced ordinary taxes." Moreover, even after naturalization, they were free from military service for another ten years (articles 20–21).[2] Thus, there was hardly any need to become a citizen. To be sure, the campaign for naturalization of resident foreigners following the Radical revolutionary attempt in 1890 received considerable political and foreign community support; nevertheless, it did not succeed (Gandolfo 1990). Prior to the 1912 electoral reform, political elections were customarily manipulated by the ruling elite on a national or provincial level. Native-born men did not bother to vote to a considerable degree. The national average share in electoral participation rose from 21 percent of all enfranchised individuals in 1910 to 69 percent in 1912 (Cantón 1973, 45).

Even after 1912, the rate of naturalizations remained remarkably low. In 1914, only 33,219 immigrant men, or 2.25 percent of the total number of foreign-born adult men, had become naturalized, although they were normally eligible after two years of residence.[3] Was this because foreigners were absorbed in their economic concerns and the advantages of naturalization questionable or in any case slight? Or was it because in practice, naturalization procedures were quite cumbersome and the attitudes of most political groups toward new citizens were adverse? Both factors were surely involved; no doubt the former was most important.

The conservative elite parties became particularly afraid of immigrant political involvement after a number of foreign colonists took part in armed revolts staged by the Radicals (*Unión cívica radical* [UCR]) in Santa Fé in 1893. But the UCR never took an explicitly pro-immigrant stand, as did the Socialist party. Founded in 1894, the Socialist party pleaded the cause of, largely immigrant, urban workers. On a provincial level, also, the Liga del Sur of Santa Fé came to the defense of immigrant interests in 1908. The electoral reform of 1912, providing for secret mandatory voting, was carried out by Conservative president Roque Sáenz Peña with a view toward integrating the Radical party into the political process.[4] In their rejection of fraudulent election practices, the Radicals either had tried revolutionary means (1893, 1905) or had abstained from voting. This was also why Sáenz Peña's partisans pushed through a proportional election procedure (*lista incompleta*) to assure mandates for minority parties as well. After the Radicals, led by Hipólito Yrigoyen, narrowly won the 1916 presidential elections, the Conservatives turned out to be unexpected beneficiaries.

On the provincial level, the Socialists of the Federal District (the City of Buenos Aires) were also quite successful. In 1913, they won two seats in the national Senate, apparently due to the votes of naturalized immigrants. Although in vain, a Conservative deputy then proposed more rigid naturalization procedures. In Santa Fé, the Liga del Sur was replaced in 1914 by the Progressive Democratic party (*Partido demócrata progressista* [PDP]), which also vied for and received naturalized immigrant votes. Under these circumstances, individual members of the Radical party surpassed the Conservatives in expressing their fear of and contempt for the immigrant mass. This xenophobic stance undoubtedly appealed to those native-born poor who were afraid of immigrant competition. They were part of the massive support enjoyed by the Radical party from 1916 until the Depression and the military coup of 1930.[5]

Electoral statistics for the period 1912–30 allow for a detailed analysis of political forces and trends. For the early years, they can be related to the national census of 1914; the next one, unfortunately, did not take place until 1947. Due to the uneven distribution of immigrants over the national territory and the regional varieties of party politics, however, pro- and anti-immigrant influences are best analyzed on the provincial level.

In this connection we have to recall that the 1853 Constitution, though modeled upon that of the United States, provided for an even stronger executive. The president was able to suspend constitutional rights by declaring a state of siege. While Congress was not in session, he alone could also make use of the power of "federal intervention." Thus he might dissolve an elected provincial administration and exert direct rule until a new provincial election. President Julio A. Roca (1880–86), for example, often used this device against such provincial cliques (*situaciones*) which did not submit to his will. Another oligarch president used the same device in 1906 to curb Roca's own influence in the provinces (Rock 1986, 155, 189). Even more serious, after the reform of 1912, President Yrigoyen (1916–20) abused the power of federal intervention on an even larger scale, with a total of twenty interventions (fifteen through presidential decree) against Conservative party machines (Rock 1986, 199f.).

We have chosen to study in some detail three administrative units that had a higher than average foreign population: the city of Buenos Aires (Federal District since 1880) and the provinces of Santa Fé and Mendoza. While the national average of foreign-born was 29.9 percent in 1914, these areas held 49.4, 35.1, and 31.8 percent, respectively. We hope that this study will help to advance scholarly analysis of a difficult problem—that is, the importance of foreigners as actors and images in Argentine politics.

The Province of Santa Fé: "Pampa Gringa"

Apart from the northern transition zone to the Gran Chaco wilderness, Santa Fé forms part of the humid pampa. Until the mid-nineteenth century, the province was very backward; the land was used only for traditional ranching, under tough *caudillo* rule, and was repeatedly exposed to Indian wars. In 1854, however, Justo José de Urquiza, a *caudillo* on a national level with liberal advisors, introduced the use of European immigrants for agricultural development of the province. The first immigrants were Swiss, French, and German. Later, a large majority were Italians. The first colony was that of Esperanza near the capital of Santa Fé, established in 1856. Further south, another new city, Rosario, favored by Urquiza, grew quickly. By 1872, there were thirty-one colonies with almost 14,000 inhabitants in the central parts of Santa Fé (Gianello 1978, 355). They had received generous tracts of land from the provincial government, generally through contracts with private entrepreneurs. Wheat production became the staple of the province. The volume grew from 20,000 tons in 1872 to 500,000 in 1891 (Scobie 1964, 42). The first export cargo of wheat left Rosario for Europe in 1878. The population increase of the province from 89,000 people in 1869 to 397,000 in 1895 was the highest one in Argentina. During this latter year, no less than 42 percent of the population was foreign-born (66 percent of them Italians). Of a total of 37,000 Santa Fé real estate owners, as many as 57 percent were foreigners. So were nine-tenths of the proprietors of industrial plants and 84 percent of the merchants.

The European immigrants had gone through many hardships and were accustomed to taking care of their problems. The provincial constitutions of 1872 and 1883 gave resident foreigners the right to vote and to be elected on the municipal level (Ensinck 1979, 178–80).[6] Therefore the loss of that privilege in the constitution of 1890 caused resentment. More serious, though, was the introduction of a provincial grain tax in 1891, a consequence of the national and provincial financial crisis of the previous year. It was probably not so much the tax as such that caused colonial anger as the fact that large landholding ranchers was not similarly taxed.[7] And the cattle barons of the northern and southernmost Santa Fé were the ones who so far dictated politics through fraud and the votes of obedient native peons. This is why wheat farmers of the central parts of southern Santa Fé let the UCR lure them into two consecutive abortive rebellions in 1893.[8] Even though most rebels were surely Argentine-born, their fathers more often than not were Europeans and at times fought together with their sons. The Swiss were particularly conspicuous.

The always latent hostility against the "gringos" now became acute and repression in the colonies was often severe. For some years, economic conditions were also bad. From a peak of 1.2 million tons of wheat in 1894, the harvest of 1897 hit bottom at 300,000 tons and prices fell. At the same time, however, it should be noted that wheat acreage tripled in size from 1887 to 1897, and toward 1900 a recovery set in. In 1914 the population of the province, with 900,000 people, had doubled since 1895. Rosario, with 91,600 inhabitants in 1895, had become the second city of Argentina with 222,590 inhabitants. No less than 43 percent were foreign-born. If age is also taken into account, the predominance of foreigners in Rosario was overwhelming. Out of all males, in 1906–7, 69 percent were foreign-born (Liebscher 1975, 127–28).

Still, the political hegemony of the oligarchy remained the same. In 1908, however, a new provincial political movement was born, the Liga del Sur.[9] Founded by a group of merchants in Rosario, it was especially directed against the unjust administrative-electoral system that gave the thinly populated North much more clout than the dynamic, densely populated South. Logically, it especially addressed itself to the foreigners. The league demanded that foreigners, if they had been residents for a certain period of time, owners of real estate, or parents of Argentine children, should get the franchise without further ado. In 1909, the league even gave its support to a massive strike by largely immigrant small businessmen against municipal taxation. The strike was put down with force.[10]

Santa Fé happened to become the first province where the 1912 electoral reform would be applied. The increase in the percentage of voters after the law was one of the highest in the country (56 percent since 1910). The provincial election in 1912 gave the victory to the Radicals. However, in order to analyze election results more clearly, as tried by Ezequiel Gallo and Silvia Sigal (1965), it becomes meaningful to divide the nineteen departments into three different groups: those of the pastoral, rather retarded north, those of the old agricultural center to the west of the city of Santa Fé, and those of the south with the dynamic city of Rosario and its rural hinterland (see map 7).

There, by 1914, farmers who owned their land were far fewer than in the center.[11] At the same time, the rate of foreign-born was by now considerably higher than in the rural hinterland.

As on the national level, the Radicals also won the elections in 1916. By now, the Partido Demócrata Progressista, led by Lisandro de la Torre, a maverick politician of elite background, took up a pro-immigrant stance after the demise of the Liga del Sur. In the national elections of 1920 (see graph 4), a pattern based on the socioeconomic differences described above can be especially clearly discerned.[12]

In the north the Radicals won 3:1, in the center with a little more, but in the south with merely 8.5 percent. Similarily, in 1922, the PDP defended itself best in the south. During the rest of the twenties, the Radicals as elsewhere were split up in pro- and anti-Yrigoyen factions. Still the Santafesino PDP did not win provincial elections until shortly after the military coup unseating former president Yrigoyen in 1930.

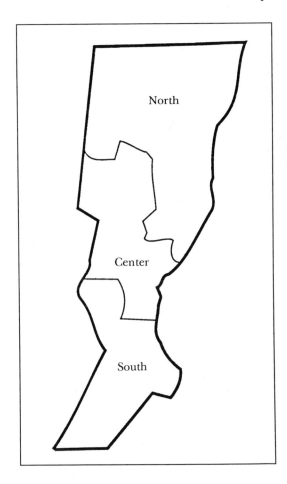

Map 7. Santa Fé,
Argentina: Distribution
of Foreign-born
Persons, 1914.
Provincial average:
32.98%; regional
averages: north:
22.21%; center:
35.09%; south:
39.98%.
Sources: Geographical
division from Gallo
and Sigal 1965;
data from Tercer
Censo 1914

By then, of course, immigration and the percentage of foreigners had
no real importance in politics any longer. Whereas in 1914, the share
of foreign-born had been 35.1 percent, the next census, in 1947, placed
them at merely 13.1 percent.

In general terms, however, the Santa Fé experience clearly shows
the relationship between party and nationality. The armed uprising
against northern political dominance in 1893 was recruited among the
agricultural settlers in the center. Even after elections had been
cleaned, the UCR continued to have its main support there, among
second- or third-generation descendants of immigrants. As claimed by
Gallo and Sigal, the correlation between the percentage of Radical votes

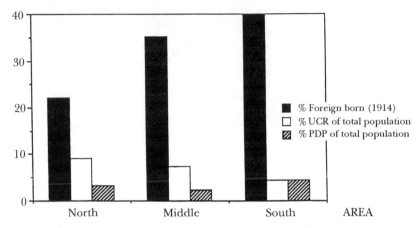

Graph 4. Santa Fé: Elections of 1920 by Area.

and shares of foreign-born in the districts of Santa Fé around 1914 was a negative one, −0.44. On the other hand, that between the PDP and the foreign-born was 0.70 (Gallo and Sigal 1965, 154).[13] It is certainly very clear that the Liga del Sur and the PDP had their main support in the South, where foreign-born merchants as well as urban proletarians and landless rural tenants and workers formed a larger population share than elsewhere.

The City of Buenos Aires: Immigrant Metropolis

From Independence onward, Buenos Aires and its widespread province, on the one hand, and most of the rest of the country, on the other, were engaged in a lengthy struggle impeding political consolidation. In 1880, however, the city was finally made a federal district, separate from the province, whereby the tricky issue was finally resolved. As the city was by far the main harbor and soon the nodal point of a quickly expanding railroad net, its growth was exceptionally quick. With 187,000 inhabitants in 1869 and 664,000 in 1895, it had no less than 1,576,000 in 1914.[14] Its share of the national population had thus grown from 12 to 13 percent in 1869 to 20 percent in 1914. By that time, the "commercial-bureaucratic" city, as historian James Scobie (1972) calls it, had also become an important center of light industry with, in 1908, 33 percent of all Argentine industrial plants, 37 percent of all industrial workers (118,435), and 37 percent, also, of the total industrial capital. The number of workers had grown to 149,289 in 1913.

Buenos Aires was already a city of immigrants in the nineteenth century: in 1869, 49.3 percent of the population was foreign-born, in 1895, 52 percent, in 1914, 50.6 percent.[15] In 1947, when finally the next census was taken, it recorded 3 million within the federal district with another 2 million outside its borders in the province.[16] The share of foreign-born had then dropped to 23.4 percent. The shares of foreign-born male adults were, as usually is the case, considerably higher.[17] Notwithstanding this excess of males among the immigrants, they clearly preferred to marry within their respective ethnic group. Buenos Aires was no "melting pot," it appears.[18]

The impact of immigration, as sociologist Gino Germani has shown (1955, 1968), was especially strong if social classes are brought into the picture. In 1914, out of a total working population of 400,000, no less than three-fourths were foreign-born. Within the lower ranges of the middle class, as many as four-fifths of 40,000 petty manufacturers and shopkeepers were foreign-born, too. On the other hand, free professions and administration were mostly recruited from among first-generation Argentines,[19] whereas old Argentines formed the elite. In an attempt at greater precision, Scobie observes that among this upper stratum known as *gente decente*, the share of the foreign-born dropped from 30 percent in 1909 to merely 19 percent in 1914. With respect to the middle stratum of petty bourgeoisie and employees, it rose slowly from 64 to 66 percent. Within the working class, during the same period of time, it rose quickly from 67 to no less than 86 percent.[20] The few people who came from Europe with good manners and wealth could make it directly into the category of *gente decente*. For "social climbers" within the mass of immigrants, on the other hand, practically nobody was able to make it. It was at best a three-generational achievement (Scobie 1974, 212–16, 273, 295f.).

In spatial terms, broadly speaking, rich people lived in the north, the middle strata lived in the west and the center, and poor people lived in the south of the city. Immigrants were spread out everywhere, but somewhat different ethnic patterns (known to us as of 1909) can be discerned (see map 8).

Since the 1880s, city planning on the Paris model had created a huge and magnificent center. By 1914, however, Buenos Aires was interspersed with many crowded slums (*conventillos*) with mostly immigrant inhabitants. By that time, the earlier mass killers, yellow fever and cholera, had been curbed, but about a fifth of the population suc-

Map 8. City of Buenos Aires by Election District, 1918. 1, Veléz Sarsfield; 2, San Cristóbal Sud; 3, Santa Lucía; 4, San Juan Evangelista; 5, Flores; 6, San Carlos Sud; 7, San Carlos Norte; 8, San Cristóbal Norte; 9, Balvanera Oreste; 10, Balvanera Sud; 11, Balvanera Norte; 12, Concepción; 13, Monserrat; 14, San Nicolás; 15, San Bernardo; 16, Belgrano; 17, Palermo; 18, Las Heras; 19, Pilar; 20, Socorro.
Source: Walter 1977, 61

cumbed to tuberculosis. As two-thirds of the immigrants were men, it is no wonder that prostitution thrived (see graph 5).

Between 1887 and 1912, the city's population had tripled but the number of crimes was reported to have increased seven times. This increase was easy to blame on the foreigners. However, while foreign-born adults were almost four-fifths of the adult population, they prob-ably committed only two-thirds of the crimes (Solberg 1970, 96f.). The generation gap was wide between the immigrants, who more often than not remained hard-working and poor, and their children, who quickly

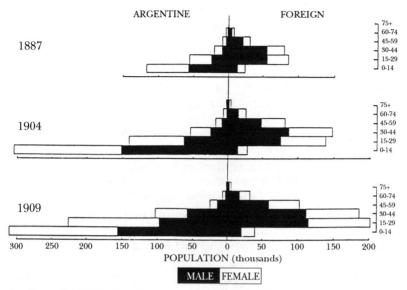

Graph 5. City of Buenos Aires: Age Pyramids, 1887, 1904, 1909: Argentines and Foreigners.
Source: Data compiled from the municipal censuses of Buenos Aires for 1887, 1904, and 1909; Scobie 1972, 1037.

adopted the local *porteño* slang and habits. It was easy for them to look at their "clumsy" parents with disdain (Scobie 1972, 1067).

In the 1880s, immigrant labor leaders of Anarchist as well as Socialist persuasions organized early unions and strikes. It has long been assumed that anarchism possessed special appeal for immigrants from impoverished but agitated Andalusia and southern Italy and thus made the early labor movement in Argentina particularly aggressive. A recent student has found this notion greatly exaggerated, though, at least prior to 1900 (Korzeniewicz 1989). Those who led the strike wave of 1895–96 were mainly Socialists. However, under Juan B. Justo, the Socialist party (*Partido socialista* [PS]), which had been formed in the mid-80s after the failure of the strikes, found political struggle more promising in the long run in improving the workers' lot than strikes. Justo appears to have been inspired mainly by Australia and New Zealand, and the party came to represent a mild variety of reformist socialism (Rock 1975b, 73). Logically, he and other Socialist leaders did all they could to urge foreign workers to become naturalized. They were only modestly successful. As late as 1914, the share of naturalized male adults among all resident aliens in Buenos Aires was merely 2.3 percent, and that was by far the highest percentage in the country (Germani 1968, 272).[21]

In the early 1900s, anarchists no doubt were instrumental in promoting strikes in the Buenos Aires labor market. When a general strike in 1902 threatened to halt grain exports, Congress at once passed the so-called Ley de Residencia. It gave the executive branch the authority to "order the expulsion of any foreigner whose conduct threatens national security or disturbs public order" (Solberg 1970, 9–11; see also figures 2–3).

Still, strikes continued. Interestingly, at the same time that the authorities tried to suppress anarchism, the problems also began to make them aware of what was called the "social question." A Conservative politician presented a bill for a labor code in 1904. Both industrialists and, after hesitation, the PS helped to defeat it, however (Walter 1977, 83–87). Between 1907 and 1910, labor unrest in Buenos Aires reached a culmination, with 775 strikes and more than 200,000 strikers. Some workers were killed by the police, so that both the anarchist labor federation, Federación obrera regional argentina (FORA), and the socialist one, Unión general de trabajadores (UGT), entered the conflict. The assassination of a hated police chief by a young anarchist and the chauvinist orgy triggered by the 1910 centennial celebration, among other events, led to the so-called Ley de Defensa Social being passed. It forbade the entrance into Argentina "of anarchists and other persons who profess or preconceive an attack . . . against public officials or governments in general." The elastic character of the law was exceedingly clear. The anarchists received a crucial blow and strikes diminished momentarily (see graph 6).[22]

In 1904, election district 4, La Boca, crowded with workers of Italian origins, saw to it that one Socialist, Alfredo Palacios, entered the Chamber of Deputies. He helped to make the party respectable (Walter 1977, 76–92). Meanwhile, the Radicals maintained their posture of abstaining from taking part in elections. In 1905 they led an abortive coup. With the Sáenz Peña election reform of 1912, which made the ballot secret and obligatory, their intransigent posture could no longer be maintained.

In the city of Buenos Aires the share of voters did in fact increase from 23 percent in 1910 to 84 percent in 1912 (Cantón 1973, 45). Nowhere were Argentine voters better prepared for the 1912 reform. There was no fraud at all, the electorate was politically aware, and more than 96 percent of the registered voters were literate. The turnout was 15 to 20 percent higher than in the interior, where literacy was also much lower. Moreover, the federal district, as such, could not be subject to federal interventions, at times used for shady purposes.[23] The UCR had succeeded in building up a very efficient party organization on district and circuit levels, a "machine" under local bosses, rewarded and

Figure 2. "The Residence Law"

Argentina (man): I'm here to get immigrants, but from now on, you'll
    have to give me selected ones only, because I don't want agitators,
    revolutionaries, strikers, Communists, socialists, anarchists. . . .
Europe (woman): That's enough; I know what you want—an immigra-
    tion composed purely of bankers and archbishops.
Source: Solberg 1970, 113. From *Cara y Caretas* (to January 1903), vol. 6, n.p.

rewarding voters under a system of patronage. Moreover, Hipólito Yrigoyen himself possessed great charisma. Thus, in Buenos Aires the
UCR won the 1912 elections with 34.4 percent of the vote, as compared
to 31.1 percent for the Socialists. Now also Justo became a national

Figure 3. Looking for a Citizenship Card

Judge: Do you swear faithfully to obey the national constitution?

Immigrant (in broken Spanish): But of course!

Judge: Are you acquainted with the constitution?

Immigrant: But of course! I know that square and even the railroad station on it!

Source: Solberg 1970, 113. From *Cara y Caretas* (20 June 1908), vol. 11, n.p.

deputy. Socialists won the 1913 by-elections with a total of 48,000 votes. President Sáenz Peña had to calm down the fears of his Conservatives that it was not the question of a foreign takeover. After all, there were no more than 13,300 naturalized foreigners in Buenos Aires, so they hardly explained the Socialist victory. The Radicals were, however, especially bitter. Their rivals had won "with the help of immigrants without roots in the country" (Cornblit 1967, 243). Their national committee even called the PS the "amoral scum of European civilization" (Solberg 1970, 126).

For all the abuse aimed at them, the Socialists, actively and moderately represented in Congress by one senator and three deputies, won the 1914 elections with a good margin, 36.9 percent, as compared to 32.9 percent for the UCR. In the long run, however, the building up

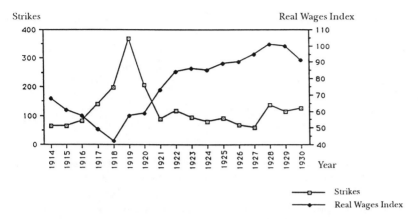

Graph 6. City of Buenos Aires: Real Wages and Number of Strikes, 1914–1930.
Sources: Based on data in Bagú 1969, 96, and referred to in Rock 1975b, 220.

of the Radical "machine" with a large network of functionaries, which had no counterpart on the Socialist side, and their nationalist, vaguely progressive message to middle-class voters, largely children of immigrants, proved more successful than did the efforts of the Socialists. The latter were decisively hampered by the fact that the foreign-born worker majority did not naturalize on a significant scale.[24] The Socialists split in 1915, when the more nationalist-minded Palacios formed his own party, the Partido socialista argentina (PSA), also hurt them. Thus, the UCR won the 1916 deputy elections with 47.1 percent over the PS with 33.3 percent and the PSA with 26.9. Henceforth, the UCR, with few exceptions (1918, 1924, 1930), dominated Buenos Aires, as they did the country.

Still, even during the 1910s, the linkages between workers, immigrants, and PS electoral strength remained strong. Within the city, on the whole, Italians and Spaniards were concentrated downtown where population was most dense, land prices high, and socialism relatively strong. In the low-priced western periphery and in Flores, Argentines were in the majority in 1914. Here, the UCR was especially strong. But that was also the case along the lower Rivadavia Street, where land prices were very high, indeed, and particularly many Spaniards lived (see map 8).

In 1915, the principal labor federation, FORA, was captured from the anarchists by the syndicalists, a more pragmatic force. At the same time as economic conditions deteriorated toward the end of the world war, the syndicalists built up a number of well-functioning unions. Also, the President himself intervened in conflicts to the benefit of labor. At the end of the world war, however, in Buenos Aires, as in so many other parts of the world, the confrontations between striking workers and police increased. Such a clash in January 1919 unleashed a wave of terror against workers and Jews, who were for many people synonymous with "communists." Hundreds were killed, many more injured and jailed. This "Semana Trágica" was tragic, indeed, especially because the right-wing extremist "vigilantes," who were especially guilty of cruelties and bloodshed, now proudly formed a so-called Argentine Patriotic League, with thousands of members.[25] After this tragic strike, unionization and new strikes mushroomed, but the government became increasingly chilly.[26] Instead, in competition with the League, its nationalist stance increased. During the twenties, real wages increased rather steadily for workers and, except for 1924, strikes declined.

Immigration had been interrupted by the World War but then it recovered. During the presidency of Marcelo I. de Alvear (1922–28), no less than 2,013,000 immigrants entered Buenos Aires and the country. However, only 31.7 percent stayed. Most of the rest must have been *golondrinas* (Pérez Amuchástegui 1965, 405). Radicals normally won the elections, apart from 1924, when the break between Yrigoyen's and Alvear's partisans could not but help the Socialists. Their record was about the same in the municipal elections, albeit by then propertied resident aliens were also allowed to vote. But they were few, merely 13,000 to 14,000.[27]

After 1920 there was a breakdown of the Socialist cadre in Buenos Aires. There were 3,659 members, 38 percent of whom were artisans and shopowners, 32 percent employees, and only 20 percent workers. Professionals, important as they were in the leadership, formed another 8 percent (Walter 1977, 175). The real shock for the Buenos Aires Socialists came in 1928, when the old Yrigoyen was overwhelmingly reelected to the presidency against "Antipersonalist Radicals." The Socialists were also split, and their old leader Juan B. Justo died in early 1928. Thus, Independent Socialists (Partido socialista internacional [PSI]), thanks to a more nationalist stance on the petroleum nationalization issue, defeated the old PS party. In the March 1930 elections, the PSI, with 36.7 percent of the vote, even defeated Yrigoyen-led UCR (with 27.9 percent) as well as the old PS (27.9 percent). But the triumph was short-lived: in September the President was ousted by a military coup and a dictatorial regime was installed. Since then, election figures, with few exceptions, have had little to say until a few years ago.

The impact of immigrants on demography and society was nowhere greater in Argentina than in Buenos Aires. For a long time, they were the majority of the working class. Since the mid-1890s, one political party, the Socialists, very consistently favored labor. Yet, though the Socialists urged immigrant workers to become citizens, their response remained weak. Nevertheless, a correlation between immigrant neighborhoods and election results can be discerned. Most Italian and Spanish immigrants lived in the south; Italians were also concentrated in San Bernardo in the north. The correlation between Italian-born residents in 1909 and the Socialist vote in 1914 was fairly high ($r = .6451$). At the same time, the correlation between foreigners and high land prices is very striking ($r = .8415$). This was so because most foreigners were crowded in the *conventillos* in the high-density districts in the south (notwithstanding the low land prices in San Bernardo with its many Italians). Not surprisingly, to take the 1916 elections, the Socialists clearly appealed to the workers ($r = .60058$), while the correlation between workers and Radical votes was highly negative ($r = -0.731148$).[28]

If, on the city level, the PS position remained very strong, naturalizations on a significant scale would have made it undefeatable. Immigrant workers instead turned their energies to unionism, where they were unhampered by any naturalization clause.[29] Though sources give ethnic breakdowns only rarely, the immigrant workers must have formed the bulk of both Anarchist and Socialist unions, and, perhaps to a lesser degree, they were important also among the syndicalists. In turn, the conflicts in the labor market at times led to sharp political confrontations between the Socialists, on one side, and the Conservatives and Radicals on the other.

The Radicals, to begin with, practically ignored the immigrants themselves. Their fiery nationalist message appealed to many of the first-generation Argentines, especially within the professions and the public sector; this was the outcome of immigrant intergenerational upward social mobility and attainment of positions reachable by means of state patronage. Thanks to their strong base organization, the Radicals won the presidential elections of 1916, though narrowly, and became the leading political force even in Buenos Aires. Now in control of a modern state, whose infrastructural power in Latin American terms was exceptionally strong, President Yrigoyen wanted to replace "class struggle" (on the Socialist model) with "class alliance," and he framed pro-labor legislation. The "Tragic Week" of 1919, however, which revealed the government to be surprisingly weak, let the Patriotic League extremists not only enter the streets in their hunt for victims, but national politics as well. After immigration stopped during World

War I (apart from anti-Semitism, always a latent tool for chauvinists), the image of foreigners seems to have lost its previous importance in Socialist-Radical politics.

The Province of Mendoza: Wine, Immigrants, and Politics

At the height of no less than 3,987 meters, the Uspallata Pass has been the main link between Chile and Argentina for a long time. Spaniards passed through it eastward to found the city of Mendoza at the foot of the Andes in 1561. The people of Mendoza, with San Juan to the north and San Luis to the east (forming together the region of Cuyo), would sustain themselves by selling their produce and cattle from the pampas in Chile. Tired travelers from Buenos Aires on their way to Chile found Mendoza a pleasant but faraway oasis with its orchards, fruit, and wine for local consumption, and alfalfa pastures to fatten the cattle bound for Chile. Three hundred years after its foundation, the city of Mendoza was wiped out by an earthquake, but it would soon function once again. There is no doubt that the decisive change toward a better-off society came with the railroad. By 1875, the rails only reached Villa Mercedes in San Luis. Yet the railroad did stimulate trade with expanding but distant Rosario. In any case, Mendocinos could now guess what would come. In 1885 their city was finally linked by railroad to Buenos Aires.[30]

As late as 1883, there were only 2,700 hectares producing grapes and 1,482 *viñateros* (wine growers), only 33 of whom had 10 or more hectares (Fleming 1987, 56). By 1895, the area had increased to 11,753 hectares; by 1908, to more than 30,000. By 1914, vineyards covered a total of 70,467 hectares divided into 6,160 properties. By far most of them (5,250) were, indeed, quite small (25 hectares and less), but 31 properties were more than 500 hectares (ibid., 118). This whole explosive growth turned grapes and wines into the basis of Mendoza's economy and society and tied it firmly to the swelling coastal market. From 1905 to 1912, figures on wine exported from Mendoza show an impressive trend. In 1905, 136,125 tons were exported; in 1908, 199,185; and in 1911, as much as 275,961 (Fleming 1987, 82; these data fit quite well with the immigration curve, see graphs 7 and 8).

European wines were still imported for the rich, but immigrant workers from the Mediterranean drank Mendozan wines. The fact that the railroad, thanks to a 3,165-meter-long tunnel through the Cordillera in 1910, finally linked Chile and Argentina did not alter Mendoza's dependence on Buenos Aires and the coast.

In turn, Mendoza's formidable economic growth was made possi-

Immigration

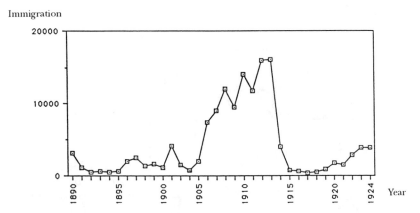

Graph 7. Immigration to Mendoza, 1890–1924.
Sources: Scobie 1988, 149 (1890–1922); Rodríguez 1979, 179 (1922–24)

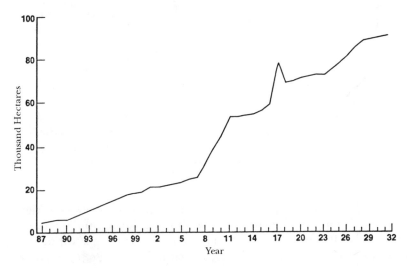

Graph 8. Mendoza: Area Cultivated with Vineyards, 1887–1931.
Source: Salvatore 1986, 58

ble by a great influx of European immigrants around 1890. During the period 1906–13, the high annual level of about 12,000 immigrants was reached. In 1895, no more than 14 percent of Mendoza's 116,000 inhabitants had been foreigners. By far most of them were Chileans. By

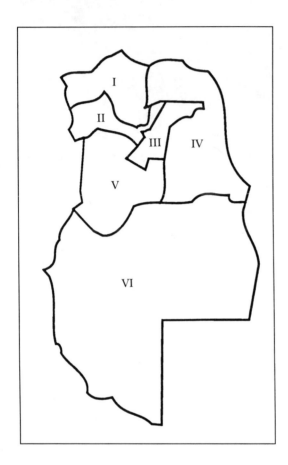

Map 9. Mendoza, by Areas, 1914. I, Greater Mendoza—Capital, Godoy Cruz, Guaymallén, Las Heras; II, Outer Ring—Luján, Maipú; III, East—Junín, Rivadavia, San Martín; IV, Northeast—La Paz, Lavalle, Santa Rosa; V, Westcenter—San Carlos, Tunuyán, Tupungato; VI, South—San Rafael, including General Alvear. Malargüe. *Source:* Tercer Censo 1914

1914, on the other hand, 32 percent of the 278,000 inhabitants of Mendoza were foreigners and now almost all were Europeans.[31] The importance of Italians, Spaniards, and other immigrants within the grape-and-wine sector had increased even more. In 1895, foreigners controlled only 29 percent of 1,770 vineyards; in 1914, they controlled 52 percent of no less than 6,160 vineyards. Wine production underwent as much as a tenfold increase between 1895 and 1914. In the latter year, immigrants formed the highest shares of the population in the northeast and south of the province (see map 9).

That was also where vineyards were most numerous. In San Rafael in the south, population and viticulture were still on the increase.

From the 1880s onward, the scarcity of qualified rural labor generated by the growth of viticulture led to the development of a special labor-tenancy contract system in Mendoza. According to one variety, the landowner would let a *contratista* plant a plot of land with vines, taking care of them for a period of three years. In the course of the term, he would receive tools, plants, and other inputs as well as advances from the landowner. At the end of the term, the benefits of the *contratista* would be calculated on the basis of 10 centavos per plant. Other contracts were based on a payment to the *contratista* based on the area under cultivation in addition to a special harvest compensation. According to Ricardo Salvatore (1986), this new intermediate rural category would be overwhelmingly filled by immigrants, not natives, whether because early, skilled immigrants did not accept work as simple peons or because landowners preferred them to less reliable native workers who used to be cattle hands. On the other hand, *contratista* farmers hired natives as seasonal labor. For the *contratistas* themselves, the system often provided a ladder to full ownership.

Wine production units, *bodegas,* were set up in close relation to the vineyards. In 1895, foreigners had owned 28 percent of the 429 *bodegas* then in existence (Supplee 1988, 304). From the 1880s onward, the capital to expand the vineyards and to construct the *bodegas* both derived from commerce. A local entrepreneur, Tiburcio Benegas, established the first modern *bodega* in the 1880s (Balán 1978, 46f.). Immigrants who arrived in Mendoza started as workers or *contratistas,* then often bought small vineyards. Many were able to expand their lands and also became *bodegueros.* By 1914, the production value of the wine industry of Mendoza was responsible for 75 percent of all industry of the province and 79 percent of the total value of wine production in Argentina. The *bodegueros* of Mendoza (1,507) had more than trebled since 1895 (when there were 423), and at least 69 percent of them were foreigners. Moreover, out of the nine *bodegueros* who in 1914 produced more than 30,000 hectoliters each, the three leaders, Tomba, Giol, and Arizú, producing more than 100,000 each, were immigrants who had started as small *viñateros* in the 1880s. Interestingly, among the employees of the *bodegas,* the nationality proportion was reversed. Foreigners were only 40 percent and their share of women and children much lower (9.7 as compared to 23.3 percent). Within the wine industry of Mendoza, the relationship between economic class and foreign nationality was obviously quite strong (see table 3 and graph 9).

In fact, in Mendoza foreigners dominated the whole industrial sector with 74 percent of all industrial owners. Their domination within the commercial sector was the same.

As elsewhere in the interior, there were extremely few naturalizations. Compared to their brethren in central Santa Fé and Buenos

Table 3. The Wine Industry of Mendoza, 1914

	1914 data	Mendozan Wine Industry (%)	
		As Share of Total Argentinian Wine Industry	As Share of Total Mendozan Industry
Number of *bodegas*	1,507[a]	34.9	59.0
Capital (in pesos)	149,039,428[b]	81.6	87.6
Production value (in pesos)	67,075,937	78.6	75.2
Number of owners	1,507	34.9	60.0
Number of foreign owners	1,024	46.0	54.0
Number of employees	7,530	46.0	
Number of foreign employees	2,981	67.1	
Value of raw material (in pesos)		75.1	73.8
Power potential (in horsepower)		75.4	

Notes: [a]An increase of 256.3 percent over 1895 figures.
    [b]An increase of 1,030.6 percent over 1895 figures.
Source: Tercer Censo 1914, vol. 7.

Aires, by far most immigrants had arrived only some years before the 1912 election reform. It would therefore be easy to dismiss them as a factor in Mendozan politics. This is hardly so, as we shall see, but their action was subtle and is hard to pin down.

Traditional politics in Mendoza was a family play. Prior to 1912, a small number of upper-class families controlled political life. As James Scobie has shown, however, this elite had for long been surprisingly open toward well-behaved foreigners. He finds the southern European share of the heads of upper-class households to be 7 percent in 1869, 17 percent in 1895, and probably even higher in 1914 (1988, 142).[32] Mendocinos had for long tried to attract immigrants, but prior to the railroad and viticultural opportunities without much success. When arriving en masse, the immigrants were well received, especially when bringing with them viticultural or technical skills.

Until at least 1914, provincial government was strictly autocratic with the aim of promoting material progress at all cost. Foreigners were

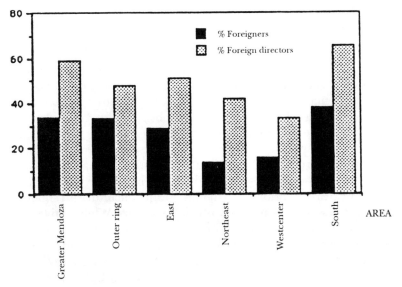

Graph 9. Foreign Population and Managers of Vineyards in Mendoza, 1914
Source: Tercer Censo 1914

most welcome if they served that aim. The economic involvement of the provincial government, from the 1880s onward, as underscored by Supplee (1988), mainly concerned the distribution of water, finances, and wine. The first years of the twentieth century were quite difficult. From 1901 to 1903 the wine industry suffered a crisis from oversupply as well as quality deficiences. The number of *bodegas* was reduced by half (Fleming 1987, 75). In 1905, as elsewhere, there was a revolutionary attempt by the Radicals to seize power but it was easily suppressed. At this time, the most powerful politician was Emilio Civit (1850–1920), a protégé of President Julio A. Roca, who became governor of Mendoza, 1907–10. He would be especially active in promoting the interests of the immigrants, whom he often praised. During the period 1902–11—that is, coinciding with the peak of immigration—more than 23 million hectares of land were sold in Mendoza, more than in any other province of the country. The number of landholders increased from 6,700 in 1901 to 18,000 in 1915 (Fleming 1987, 121f.). Even more crucial was Civit's granting of large-size water rights. This was so in particular in the far-flung San Rafael department in the south with the Diamante and Atuel rivers. This was a way of winning influential supporters, some of them immigrants, of course (Heaps-Nelson

1977, 10–13). Under Civit, a very numerous police force helped to maintain "peace." After Roca left the presidency in 1904, one of his successors, Figueroa Alcorta, was far from pleased with Civit, but Civit somehow escaped federal intervention. Instead he was able to impose his chief of police as a new governor, with the support of "almost all the province's major wine producers" (Peck 1977, 146).[33] Elected a national senator himself, Civit soon left Buenos Aires for Paris.

In Civit's absence, his political machine collapsed. Civit, apparently, had been supported mainly by the foreign *bodegueros*. American student Supplee (1988, 388) declares that "a native-immigrant split did exist (in the wine sector). Native producers were used to participating in the political arena. Prior to Civit, immigrant viniculturists remained politically quiescent and held few official positions. While native producers formed the political opposition to achieve their economic ends, foreigners operated as an interest group and lobbied the administration in power to achieve its economic goals." Her thesis seems likely but hard to prove. After Civit, the new governor, Rafael Ortega, Jr., soon got into trouble with the large *bodegueros* and their organization, Sociedad de Vitivinicultores de Mendoza (SVM). Above all, they resisted the provincial government's attempt to raise the tax on wine exports. Instead, they helped finance the next election campaign against Ortega. Merchants, largely foreigners, also fought against tax increases through their Liga de defensa comercial (Peck 1977, 153–58). Together, *bodegueros* and shopkeepers were behind the triumph of the new Partido popular (PP) in 1912. In the first more or less "clean" elections, 1914, the same party got its candidate elected governor. However, by now the whole wine industry, once again, found itself in a deep crisis, with overproduction and dropping prices. The efforts of the provincial government to intervene to defend prices were costly but hardly successful. In the course of the crisis, moreover, large and small *bodegueros* suffered a political split.

While the Conservatives—that is, Civit and the PP—enjoyed the support of the CVM, the Radicals, encouraged by the national triumph of Yrigoyen, were supported by a new organization of small wine producers, Centro de bodegueros. Hard-hit grape growers were also among the supporters of the Radical candidate, José Néstor Lencinas, a charismatic leader once involved in the revolution attempt of 1905. In fact, positive correlation can be found ($r = 0.6028$) between foreign-born and UCR votes in the 1916 elections. After Yrigoyen made a federal intervention in his favor, Lencinas won the elections in 1918. Among quite a few conflicts during his term as governor, the one with the new organization of wine- and grape producers, Compañía Vitivinícola, was especially serious. He made it clear that he detested that a few *gringos bodegueros* tried to organize their workers against him (Rodríguez 1979, 105). When Lencinas tried to dissolve the company, the provincial Supreme Court condemned his action. In turn, this led to a lengthy federal intervention and a personal break between Yrigoyen and Lencinas. The latter organized his own Lencinista Radical Party. José Néstor died in early 1920, but in 1922 his young, equally charismatic son, Carlos Washington, with his UCR Lencinista, won an electoral triumph over the other parties, including Yrigoyenista Radicals. The tension continued, however, with the federal government, which intervened repeatedly in the affairs of Mendoza.[34]

Behind this interventionism was probably, as David Rock suggests, among other things, a wish to support Buenos Aires consumer interests during inflation by switching the burden to politically weaker provinces in the interior (1975b, 114f., 247–49). Obviously, the local interests most adversely affected in Mendoza were those of wine producers. After having voiced this protest against interventionism, Lencinas, Jr., on his return to Mendoza, was murdered in 1929. According to Rock (ibid., 249f.), Radical shock troopers (Klan Radical) were responsible (compare Rodríguez 1979, 322–29). As leaders, both father and son had been dynamic, and some social reformist measures were actually carried out. Yet, their often ruthless behavior had caused continuous conflicts both within the province itself and with Buenos Aires.

What was then the role of the foreigners in Mendozan politics? As in most parts of Argentina, the Socialist party was the only one consistently pro-immigrant. In Mendoza, though, the only sizeable group was the one in the capital, where they gathered between 500 and 1,500 votes (Cantón 1968/69, 1, passim; Walter 1977, 129). The political clout of the foreigners was more complex but quite important. They seem to have dominated both among the large and the small *bodegueros*, pressure groups of basic importance even though increasingly, due to different economic and tax interest, they would split politically.[35] Foreigners were also, surely, influential among the almost 4,000 *viñateros* without any *bodegas* and with mostly very small lots of land. Foreign-born in both categories collaborated with native-born, and they did not conduct any special ethnic policy. By far most did not bother to become naturalized.[36] It is a fact, however, that they made up a majority share in the wine industry, and it was around that industry that provincial politics revolved.

Naturally, the *gringos* were especially visible from below. In a novel from 1942, *Alamos talados*, Abelardo Arias highlights the conflict between poor but proud *viñateros* and the mighty *gringos bodegueros* in San

Rafael (for example, Arias 1943, 153). This was the department where Civit had made some wealthy people even more rich and where the share of foreign landowners (47 percent) was higher in 1914 than anywhere else in Mendoza.[37]

The three Argentine cases studied here—that is, the provinces of Santa Fé and Mendoza and the city of Buenos Aires—represent profoundly different varieties of the same theme: foreigners in politics within the frame of the 1853 Constitution and subsequent national legislation. The most direct type of foreigner participation in politics was that of Santa Fé. After settlers in the "colonies" lost their original autonomy and their right to vote on the municipal level, they rose in rebellion in 1893. After the election reform law of 1912, their cause was pleaded by pro-immigrant regional parties. Mendoza represents an opposite case. Here overseas immigration was late and rapidly integrated with the booming grape-and-wine sector but on different levels. Immigrants then used their strong economic position to support existing political parties favoring their respective interests by means of their professional organizations. While large wine producers would support the Conservatives, small wine growers instead favored the domestic variety of radicalism. Mendoza also illustrates how the national state replaced its traditional use of "despotic power" against opponents in the interior with the rather bland, infrastructural use of federal interventions. The case of Buenos Aires, finally, is quite distinct. As a federal capital, its politics took place at the very core of the nation. Here the Socialist party consistently defended the rights of immigrant workers. On the other hand, they themselves above all conducted their fight on the level of unions in frequent clashes with the forces of repression.

CHAPTER 7

Conclusions

I HAVE TRIED to highlight state policies and regional reactions to such policies by means of a series of studies comparing different regions. That is, I have been concerned with spatial perspectives. But it is, of course, also possible to consider the themes in a more general temporal perspective. Consequently, in these concluding remarks I shall first take up the synchronical dimension of each theme, then the diachronical one.

To begin with, however, I should rephrase and summarize my own view on the state over time in Latin America. I certainly deny that the state is a mere "tool" or "expression" of one particular class. I think continuous interplay between the state and civil society is what really matters. Through a state elite it tries to impose power, be it, in Mann's terms, "despotic" or "infrastructural," on that society. Spanish and Portuguese America were the colonial domains of two pioneering European national states, the power of which were stronger overseas in some respects (e.g., with respect to the control over the church), in other respects, for several reasons, weaker than in the metropolitan country. Consequently, Independence meant a profound change when national states emerged. This was so, even though these states were preconditioned by the eighteenth-century administrative reforms and civil society still retained considerable continuity. Since then, each of the Latin American states has undergone a series of transformations, characterized by different forms and degrees of "despotic" (*caudillismos*) and infrastructural power. On the whole in Latin America the new states did precede their nations. On the other hand, nation-states in Latin America, indeed, appeared early when compared to most European nation-states of today.

With respect to the attempts of the Spanish state to impose ethnic dualism, as expressed by the terms of "República de los españoles" and "República de los indios," and to keep them as far as possible apart from each other, the failure of such policies has been illustrated by three regional studies. My choice was the region of Tlaxcala in New Spain/Mexico, that of Tunja in New Granada/Colombia, and, finally, the region around the Alto Parana and Uruguay rivers in the eastern part of Rio de la Plata/Argentina, Paraguay, Rio Grande do Sul with the famous thirty Jesuit missions among the Guaraní Indians.

In the wake of the Conquest, the Indian city-state of Tlaxcala had been granted far-reaching autonomy by the Spanish state, and its population was averse to non-Indian penetration. Therefore, it would have been reasonable to expect that the laws imposing residential segregation could at least have been carried out there. The process of social change set in motion by the simultaneous decline of the Indian population and the rapid increase of landless mestizos, however, simply proved too strong. From the seventeenth century onward, the presence of a substantial non-Indian population in the city and the surrounding countryside was an irreversible fact. This was so even though an Indian majority continued to exist there until the early twentieth century.

In Tunja, on the other hand, the process of rural mestization went on almost unhampered by the repeated attempts of the authorities to impose the segregation laws. Paradoxically, however, in the late eighteenth century, the laws were used, in a perverted sense, not to protect the Indians from non-Indian encroachments, as they were intended to, but to drive out Indian minorities from now heavily mestizo-dominated communities.

Unlike Tlaxcala and Tunja, the Jesuit missions were situated in a peripheral border region. Here, with minor modifications, the segregation laws were, indeed, applied for as long as the Jesuit fathers remained in control, that is, until 1767–68. This policy was simply quite in line with the far-reaching de facto autonomy of their Guaraní missions, which the Jesuits, thanks to their skillful diplomacy, had been able to obtain from the Spanish court. However, the splendid isolation of the Guaraní missions during the Jesuit era stands out as an exception confirming the rule of the general failure of the Spanish segregation policy. After their expulsion, the isolation was very soon broken with the various consequences, "good" or "bad," to which this change was deemed to have led.

It is always very difficult to follow up how socioracial conditions in Latin America changed—or did not change—once Independence had been attained. In most of Spanish America, at least, socioracial designations vanish from our documentary sources. Similarly, in one country after another, the slave/free dichotomy disappears with the abolition of slavery. I have chosen Venezuela to illustrate the transition from the colonial "Régimen de las Castas" to legal equality and, gradually, a lessening of discrimination against the "dark-skinned" majority. I did so because discrimination during the colonial era appears to have been especially severe in Venezuela. Conflicts reflecting the hatred between the various socioracial groups played an especially great role there in the course of the protracted wars of independence.

For my account of the Venezuelan case between the eve of Independence and about 1860, I chose to compare three provinces: Cumaná, in the northeast of the country; Valencia/Carabobo, just west of Caracas; and Barinas, farther west, the bulk of which is situated in the plains of the interior (llanos).

During this period, Cumaná became increasingly marginal to the central part of the country. At the same time, the various political changes notwithstanding, it seems to have enjoyed a rather stable *caudillo* rule, and social conflicts there appear to have been relatively weak. No major social change can be discerned in the Cumaná/Sucre region. On the other hand, Carabobo, with at first its booming cocoa plantations worked by numerous African slaves, found itself, besides the province of Caracas, at the very center of political and military struggle during most of our period. At least in the long run, the terrible display of violence on the part of guerillas as well as regular troops seems to have led to a considerable degree of division of rural property. That is an important requirement of democracy in a broader sense. In far-flung Barinas, finally, the colonial patterns of socioracial stratification and discrimination did not have as deep roots as in the other two regions. Therefore, the nineteenth-century civil wars led to a crushing defeat of the landed elite. In the course of the century, Barinas became a land characterized by poor and primitive living conditions, almost regardless of race.

The backlands of Bahia and Pernambuco in northeast Brazil in the nineteenth century also were, and still remain, lands characterized by harsh and poor living conditions. In fact, the environment is even more hostile to people there than in the llanos. My study of the Quebra Quilos movement of the 1870s has no comparative ambitions. Instead, I chose to do it as a very clear illustration of a popular, regional reaction to a premature modernizing measure of the Brazilian imperial state. In this case, "region" is defined in geo-ecological terms, not in administrative terms, as in the other studies.

Finally, I move on to Argentina, of all the countries in the whole world, one of the most transformed by the phenomenon of mass immigration, to study the impact of this inflow of new people on provincial politics—that is, to search for regional reactions to the pro-immigration stance of the national state. I chose the provinces of Santa

Fé and Mendoza as well as the national capital of Buenos Aires for representing very different types of immigrant political importance, be it in an active or a passive sense. The time period chosen, 1912–30, was a natural one because only for this period do election figures make any sense. In Santa Fé, mass immigration had started early, by the mid-nineteenth century. During our period, the province represented the most clear-cut case of pro- and anti-immigration provincial politics. In Mendoza, on the other hand, mass immigration was late and somewhat less heavy than in either the city of Buenos Aires or the Santa Fé province. Yet the economic power of the immigrants in Mendoza, linked as they were to the booming wine industry, made various immigrant economic groups very strong forces behind the rather colorful provincial politics.

The city of Buenos Aires, finally, was the place where national politics were actually made and where, at the same time, immigrants were overwhelmingly numerous during our whole period. Moreover, in this city one national political party, the Socialist party, was at the same time impressively strong locally and quite ready to espouse the cause of the immigrants. This is why the failure of the immigrants to naturalize, whatever its causes, becomes especially glaring precisely in the case of the city of Buenos Aires. By making themselves citizens, they might have steered both Buenos Aires and the whole nation along a different, possibly more fortunate, political course during a crucial era. Seen from this perspective, heavy immigrant participation in union struggles in Buenos Aires appears to have mattered less.

Let me now try to place the various themes of this book into a more general temporal perspective.

To begin with, the segregation policy of the Spanish colonial state gradually took shape from about 1550 to 1650. Theoretically the legislation in question remained in force until the end of the colonial period. Even so, the chances of the colonial state to get this policy imposed—that is, to radically restrict the life conditions of the civil society, apart from certain peripheral areas under religious control—had probably vanished in the late sixteenth century (if they ever existed). Our example eloquently illustrates both the great ambition of the colonial state to mold society according to its norms as well as its complete failure to do so. The passive but successful resistance to state policies in this case both came from bureaucrats giving up their tasks and non-Indian groups simply ignoring or refusing to obey legal norms.

With respect to the so-called Society of Castes—that is, the hierarchical ordering of the various socioracial groups—the dominant social strata were even more discriminatory than the state. In Venezuela, where late colonial economic growth also threatened to unleash considerable upward social mobility of darker-skinned individuals, the discrimination on the part of the white upper stratum against the lower, more or less dark-skinned strata became particularly sharp. That is why Venezuela appeared to be an especially interesting case to study with respect to what happened after the legal bases for discrimination (in 1854, even slavery) had vanished.

To begin with, under a paternalistic yet firm national state, traditional distance was, in fact, preserved without any major complications between a still almost exclusively white upper stratum and mostly dark-skinned masses. Then, however, party strife and civil wars led to a general weakening of the white elite and to universal male suffrage in 1857–58—that is, only four years after the abolition of slavery. Practically continuous dictatorship from the 1870s onwards—a sheer display of "despotic power"—became the way in which the state nevertheless would escape from the democratic consequences of universal suffrage as well as real federalism. Social equality, as I have already explained, became more of a reality in the llanos, where caste society had been less entrenched in colonial times.

Within the Latin American context, the stability of Brazil under Emperor Pedro II (1840–89) has become proverbial. Yet research has been rather slow in uncovering the nature of the relationship between the imperial state and society on various levels. The example of a regional reaction against both the introduction of the metric system and other rationalistic features of imperial policy which we have chosen to analyze was a kind of *jacquerie* far away from imperial headquarters. The suppression eloquently shows that even the remarkably smooth government of Pedro II would not hesitate to use "despotic power" when problems arose outside its range of "infrastructural power."

Argentine society, to an extent probably unparalleled elsewhere in the world, was completely transformed by mass immigration between 1871 and 1914. How did that, in turn, affect the state and politics in general? To analyze this thorny problem, two major factors have to be kept in mind. First, political elections, traditionally determined by systematic fraud, became free in 1912, to remain so until the military coup of 1930. Second, the overwhelming majority of the immigrants never became naturalized. Thus, our analysis has necessarily been mostly indirect and rather subtle. Our sample of territorial units shows that the attitudes for or against immigration on the part of the various political parties can be traced in election results in two jurisdictions where immigration was really heavy (Federal District, Santa Fé). Yet the control of the most important economic resource of a province by a minority of immigrants (such as wine production in Mendoza) probably gave a considerable group of immigrants greater clout in politics than in any of the other two jurisdictions and, perhaps, in other Argentine provinces as well. In any case, when the period of democracy ended, immigration also practically ceased, both victims of the Depression.

It would, of course, have been easy to find further and also more recent illustrations of the relationship between state and society that lend themselves to analysis primarily on the regional level. Our sample, however, should suffice as a first experiment in this genre.

Notes

Chapter 1. Introduction: State and Region

1. The term *civil society* in English dates back to the late sixteenth century. In Scottish eighteenth-century social theory, it denoted a civilized society with a nondespotic state. For the philosopher Hegel, it formed an intermediate link between family and state (Mann 1983, 45). For a historical outline of the emergence and growing complexity of civil society in Western Europe, see Poggi (1978, 77–85). In present usage, the words normally refer to the economic, social, and other groupings and activities not actually controlled by the state. This is why Dahrendorf (1990, 95ff.) strongly emphasizes the need to rebuild civil society (or *Bürgerlich*) in Eastern Europe.

2. For Spain, this process has been analyzed, above all, by Maravall (1972). But the Empire was simply too large to permit a state formation of similar strength. In his view, there was a "desajuste entre el Imperio español y el Estado peninsular," above all the Crown of Castile, where the trends toward a unity of the state were so strong, early, and general (1:91).

3. Pietschmann (1987, 429) asks the crucial question, "si se puede hablar de un estado colonial en singular al referirse a los complejos luso e hispanoamericanos coloniales o si hay que postular ya varias entidades con carácter estatal o a lo menos protoestatal." As he rightly observes, "en este contexto reina una tremenda confusión terminológica." Moreover, the use of terms like "sociedad venezolana" with respect to the colonial period, implies "proyecciones hacia atrás desde una perspectiva postindependentista o . . . sólo responden a delimitaciones político-institucionales *por lo tanto estatales*" (my emphasis). For important distinctions, see especially Góngora (1951, 29–35, 298–310). For a critical commentary on the notion of the "colonial state," see Malamud (1991).

4. Interestingly, this did not prevent such a knowledgeable and intelligent observer as Alexander von Humboldt to react strongly against the whole idea of a colonial state. "C'est que l'idée de la Colonie même est une idée immorale," as quoted by Pietschmann (1987, 432). On the impact of the Bourbon reforms, to quote Colin MacLachlan (1988): "The Crown no longer occupied the relatively safe position made possible by its divine charge to guide the Christian community, in which the judgment of whether it succeeded or failed awaited the celestial moment. Acceptance of the new ideology made it possible for the

Bourbon state to succeed or fail, a possibility not present in the Hapsburg notion of kingship" (127).

5. For more detailed discussions of the legitimacy of the new states, see Chapter 2 below, Problemas (1984), and Annino (1987).

6. This is how I interpret Mann (1984, 1986), who barely even mentions Latin America.

7. Robinson (1979, 11–21). See also Mörner (1983, 358–61). Bronner (1986, 21f.) provides a list of Latin American conceptual interpretations of "region." I prefer Robinson's interpretation, however.

8. For a discussion of the "region" concept as applied to Latin America in strictly economic terms, see Roberts (1981, 10–20). His stress on its relationship with an uneven economic development and on the change of boundaries over time appeals to me. In the same volume, Marco Palacios (1981), however, rightly warns against predominantly "economicist" interpretations of the theme "state and region" (41). According to Carmagnani (1984, 144), anyway, during the period of the "state of the oligarchy" (ca. 1880–1914), the state did not succeed in imposing itself "de modo uniforme y orgánico en todas las regiones de un mismo país."

9. A recent comparative analysis of a variety of regional responses to "economic change" is that of Langer (1989).

Chapter 2. State and Civil Society in Latin America: A Historiographical Discussion

1. Keane (1988, 60f.) criticizes the prevailing view (represented, e.g., by Michael Mann) that it was Hegel who primarily made the distinction between state and society "a key organizing principle of the modern world." According to Keane, there were many intellectuals who during the period 1750–1850 reached similar conclusions.

2. Characteristically, the reviewer of Phelan's book (1967) in the *Hispanic American Historical Review,* J. H. Parry, did not seem to notice the importance of his "Weberian" analysis (see *HAHR* 43, 4 [1968]: 697–99). As observed by Tulio Halperín Donghi (Mitchell 1988, 230), Stuart B. Schwartz's monograph on the magistrate of Bahia (1973) was inspired by Phelan's use of Weber. He did not adopt the Weberian model, however. Pietschmann (1980b), who also knows his Weber, finds that the bureaucratic character of the Spanish American administration, for example, sales of offices notwithstanding, was clearly more important than existing patrimonial traits. With respect to Eisenstadt's "centralized historical bureaucratic empires or states," they comprise a very heterogeneous group: Egyptian, Inca/Aztec, Chinese, Roman, Byzantine, European during the Age of Absolutism, Spanish American, British colonial in India, and so forth (1963, 11). For all the reservations of the author, it is difficult to accept the usefulness of this kind of "super macro" categorization.

3. As Stepan (1978) also observes, paradoxically, while from the fifties onwards, "almost everywhere the role of the state grew, one of the few places it withered away, was in political science" (!).

4. Even such a very competent historian as Marcello Carmagnani, in his survey of state and society in Latin America, 1850–1930 (1984; original Italian ed. 1982), regards the state during this period as a mere tool of the "oligarchy."

5. H. J. König, one of the organizers of the symposium, later published a monograph (1988) in which he traces the evolution from self-consciousness to nationalism and "modernization" in New Granada/Colombia. In this country, state formation was quite complex.

6. In recent decades, the concept of "power" has become the subject of increasingly extensive debates on the part of neo-Marxists and others. In relative isolation for many years, French philosopher Michel Foucault (1926–84) worked on this subject in several books. He insisted that the state was "but one of many power relations." In particular, Foucault developed his famous theory of "power = knowledge." In 1975 he published "Discipline and Punish," a study of the prison, certainly a major agency of the state's control apparatus. Still, Foucault did not believe that the state's use of power is merely repressive. His analysis presents some traits in common with the works of the neo-Marxists, Skocpol, and others and has its very specific features. See, e.g., Lemert and Gillan (1982, 110–18).

7. In a well-known work, *Imagined Communities* (1991; first ed. 1983), Benedict Anderson (a brother of Perry's) presents a similar view (see his Chap. 4).

Chapter 3. The Segregation Policy of the Colonial State

1. This chapter is based on Mörner (1970) with only a few references to more recent studies. Ann Wightman (1990) has studied another related aspect of social change during the period until 1720—that is, the mass migration of *indios forasteros* undermining the systems of *reducciones* and of Indian compulsory labor service (*mita*). She finds crown policies on the issue "contradictory and confusing" (128f.).

2. Pietschmann (1983, 226) discusses the reasons for a decline in population between 1779 and 1793. He finds that Indians formed 72.5 percent of the total population in 1793.

3. For a long-term perspective of Tlaxcalan demographic evolution since 100 B.C., with the dramatic population drop after 1519 and the quick recovery some 100 years later, see Dumond (1976).

4. Indian resistance to nucleated settlements is also emphasized by Villamarín and Villamarín (1979) in the case of the *sabana*, or savannah, surrounding Bogotá.

5. "En cabal propiedad." The translation is from Phelan 1978, 161. His interpretation of the above term is more convincing in this case than that of Meza Lopehandía (1976, 20f.), who believes that it refers to the traditional collective form of tenure.

6. Colmenares 1970, 210–12. Fals Borda (1957, 96f.) underlines that the *resguardos* in Tunja still existing after 1800 would normally have been let out to non-Indian tenants.

Chapter 4. Dark-skinned New "Citizens" Face the Newborn National State

1. José Tadeo Monagas entered the presidency in 1847 as Páez's protégé but gradually approached the Liberals. On 24 January 1848, a violent incident took place in and outside Congress in which eight people were killed. For a contemporary account of the day which "la prensa radical se llama 'glorioso,'" see a dispatch by the Swedish Minister Adlercreutz (1928, 219f.). While historian González Guinan (1954, 411–19), for example, places most blame with the Conservatives, his younger colleague Morón (1971, 254–56) finds Monagas himself mainly responsible. In whatever case, the break between Monagas and Páez was now complete. The latter's uprising, 1848–49, ended in utter failure.

2. See Bushnell (1972, 199ff.) for details on the debate on the issue. Rodríguez (1977, 52) quotes the *Diario de los Avisos,* 24 March 1858, according to which people who owned property worth 100,000 to 200,000 pesos were found to be *riquísimos;* those who owned 20,000 to 25,000, were in any case well-off. To become an elector, according to the 1830 Constitution one should have a property rent of 200 pesos, a professional income of 300 pesos, or a salary of 400 pesos. To become a representative or a senator, the required minimal figures were 400/500/600 and 800/1,000/1,200 pesos, respectively (Gil Fortoul 1954, 3:354, 358f.).

3. In 1846, 128,785 persons possessed the franchise; 40.9 percent were farmers, 9.7 percent cattle owners, and, remarkably, no less than 33 percent *jornaleros.* Artisans, merchants, and the like held smaller shares, but their share was higher among those who actually voted.

4. On the concept of *pardo,* see Lombardi (1976, 43ff.).

5. As John Lynch (1973, 223) underscores, the patriot victory of 1821 "produced a large-scale transfer of property and a new latifundist class, without significantly modifying the social structure." According to Liberal leader A. L. Guzmán, Páez himself was "el más rico propietario del país, él de más pingües y seguras rentas" (Pino Iturrieta 1987, 75f.).

6. For 1825, estimates vary between 710,633 (Codazzi) and 785,000 (Humboldt). See Rasmussen (1947, 155). The estimates for 1810–47 in Izard (1970, 15) are bewildering, to say the least.

7. As well put by Manuel Pérez Vila in *Política* (1976, 51), "Los empleos oficiales, los altos grados militares, el acceso a las universidades ya no estaban cerrados a los pardos y mestizos, aún cuando las puertas no siempre se abrieron ampliamente ni de buen grado para ellos. El ascenso social era teóricamente posible, pero en la práctica sólo una minoría estuvo en condiciones de subir, o se atrevió [!] a intentarlo." At a concert at President Páez's, in 1831, the British minister found the lack of "distinction of either rank or colours most irritatingly disgusting" (Dupoy 1966, 574).

8. Swedish minister Adlercreutz, in an unpublished report of 12 December 1843, finds the time has arrived to "regler les conflits entre proprietaires et capitalistes; les propriétés, divisées, changeront de maitres et une classe

d'hommes riche en bien-fonds d'une valeur nominelle, se trouverá ruinée. Telle est en partie la cause de la crise financière et commercielle que souffre actuellement ce pays." Riksarkivet (National Archives) Stockholm: Kabinettet för utrikes brevväxling, "Depescher från beskickningen i Caracas, 1839–45, 1847–49."

9. According to oral tradition, gathered by Armas Chitty (1961, 162f.), in a llano town called Tucupido (Guárico), in 1862, a mulatto warrior exclaimed before being executed: "Nosotros peleamos por odio a los blancos." There is much similar evidence. Foreign observers often underlined racial conflict. See, for example, a dispatch from the French consul in Caracas on 30 August 1845, quoted by Parra-Pérez (1959–60, 2:232f.), "En un país cuya población es tan heterogénea, . . . la diferencia de razas alimenta en la gente de color un odio inveterado contra los blancos. Pero este año el partido liberal no ha temido excitar al populacho, recordarle derechos que éste parecía ignorar, inspirarle aversión contra los gobernantes."

10. According to Brazilian diplomat Lisboa (1954, 83f.), who visited Venezuela in 1852–53, members of the colonial aristocracy with such names as Toro, Tovar, and Herrera enjoyed high status and tried to marry within their circle. Yet, politically, the Toros and the Tovares were traditional rivals.

11. Within the elite, as Laureano Vallenilla Lanz observed (1919, 267), "por regla general se nacía godo o liberal"—that is, from the foundation of the Liberal Party and the newspaper "El Venezolano," led by Antonio Leocadio Guzmán from 1840 onward (González Guinan 1954, 3:140–49).

12. The classical novel *Pobre Negro* (1937) by Rómulo Gallegos has the equalization process during the Federal War as its main theme. Along similar lines, see Nava (1965, 530). Actually, the "racial harmony" of contemporary Venezuelan urban society, as in Brazil, should be taken with a grain of salt. See Wright (1988) and other studies by the same author. Moreover, as B. A. Frankel, in Política (1976, 160), puts it: "Lo que sí es seguro es, que la gente de color siguió siendo la más pobre de toda la nación."

13. As Lombardi (1985, 178) says: "Bien puede ser que los caudillos del este, especialmente Mariño, se hicieran ilusiones acerca de una Venezuela independiente, pero esa quimera resultaba menos atractiva que la idea de una Venezuela unida y controlada desde Caracas por la élite de la región oriental." Quote in text from Lombardi (1979, 463).

14. The various provincial population figures, 1800–1961, are presented and briefly discussed in Vila (1965, 139f.) and Humboldt (1970, 1:298). The 1793 estimate is summarized by McKinley (1985, 26f.). There is no counterpart for the province of Caracas. On the other hand, I have not found any breakdown of socioracial groups (*castas*) for Cumaná around 1800 similar to the data used by Lombardi (1976) for the Caracas province. To discuss the socioracial composition of the Cumanese population after Independence becomes even more difficult, if not impossible.

15. In the elections of 1846, Antonio Leocadio Guzmán received three times as many votes as José Tadeo Monagas (Parra-Pérez 1959–60, 1:363). Interest-

ingly, however, the Cumaná counterpart to Guzmán, fiery publicist Blas Bruzual, supported not him but the other Monagas brother, José Gregorio (Pérez Vila in *Política* 1976, 86f.).

16. On the role of Cumaná in early federalism in the 1850s, see, e.g., Díaz Sánchez (1950, 433ff.); Mathews in *Política* (1976, 100f.). A contemporary, Colonel Emilio Navarro (1963, 17), enhances the importance of the "sabio tribuno, columna de honra y gloria del Gran Partido Liberal, Doctor Estanislao Rendón."

17. According to Castillo Blomquist (1987, 262), "Los hombres que aprendieron luchar defendiendo el gobierno de [J. T.] Monagas se convertirían en los Federalistas de la Guerra Federal." This should refer especially to the Oriente. The militias were led by Liberal, often *pardo* officers.

18. Out of this total, 41 percent were *pardos*, 36 percent "whites," 18 percent "blacks" (83 percent slaves), and 11 percent Indians.

19. In Carabobo, the elections of 1846 were won by "fusionist" general Bartolomé Salom (García Ponce 1982, 128).

20. The start of the rebellion is vividly described by García Ponce (1982, 105–24), who finds it did not succeed because it was limited to one central area and because no Liberal leaders of first rank joined it.

21. At the same time it is worthwhile to notice that Carabobo, with 97,000 people, had the second highest population density in the country (146 inhabitants per square league) while, for instance, Cumaná, with about 51,000 inhabitants, had one of the lowest provincial densities of the nation (35 per square league). Our third province, Barinas, with 109,000 people at the time, presents a more average density (Brito Figueroa 1966, 1:263).

22. Interestingly, two days after his *pronunciamiento* of 5 March, Castro decreed that "todos los jornaleros que tomasen las armas para defender la revolución quedarían libres de sus compromisos pecuniarios por razón de trabajo personal y que la nación pagaría las cantidades que debían los sirvientes y jornaleros," according to the summary in González Guinan (1954, 6:132).

23. Why Valencia never imposed itself is discussed in Lombardi (1979, esp. 451f.). Its population actually declined from 1854 to 1873 (see table 2).

24. Humboldt (1970, 3:98f.) reports that by 1800 the production of indigo had diminished rapidly in Venezuela since 1787 and only held its own in Barinas. Excellent tobacco was also produced there but was impeded by the state monopoly on that product.

25. In his famous novel *Doña Bárbara* (1929), Rómulo Gallegos writes: "En el Llano . . . propiedad que se mueve no es propiedad." On the importance of contraband trade, see, e.g., Gosselman (1962, 148). García Müller (1986, 534) asserts, with respect to the 1830s, that "Barinas se conecta con el mercado mundial a través de la constitución de Sociedades Mercantiles con aportes de Barineses y Angostureños interconectados con la Isla de Trinidad (Británica)."

26. There are slightly different figures for 1854–55 in Rodríguez (1981, 193).

27. Among those who in the 1840s sought refuge in the llanos, according

to Izard (1981, 126), were many youngsters escaping military service and vagrants put to forced labor in agricultural districts.

28. The administration of justice on the local level is painted in dark colors in the 1830s by traveler Hawkshaw (1975, 150f.). The "Ley de azotes" was what the law was named by Liberal Tomás Lander (García Ponce 1982, 72).

29. Rodríguez (1981, 209) ties Arteaga closely to the Indios de Guanarito faction, the main agents of the illegal trade in hides, while at the same time the most militant Federalist *guerilleros*.

30. For his part, Izard (1979b, 61) enhances the importance of marginalized refugees from nuclear areas to the llanos for the recruitment of the Federalist Montoneras. He also finds (1982) these to be better provisioned with a much larger base of recruitment than government forces. Their leadership was perhaps less clear. In early 1862, the Minister of the Interior, as quoted by Izard (1987, 128), asserted that the rebels were mere "hordas desalmadas, sin fe, sin ley, sin religión y aún sin caudillo [!]." For a distinction, in turn, between caudillism and militarism which we have not taken up in this essay, see Gilmore (1964) and Pérez Vila (1984, 12).

31. According to Eastwick (1959, 188), in the 1860s the city of Barinas had only 6,000 inhabitants, while Nutrias had 6,500.

32. Vallenilla Lanz (1960, 188f.) claims that *caciquismo* prevailed above all where Negro mixture was slight. Indian ancestry prepared the soil for what he coined *federalismo de la caudillocracia*. This bold, questionable assertion could possibly apply to Barinas but not, for example, to Cumaná. Compare Concepto (1966, 43f.).

Chapter 5. The Masses Face the Modernizing Ambitions of the National State

1. For example, historical geographer Galloway (1971) is convinced that it was the Empire that "managed to weld Portuguese America into a single nation" (356).

2. The debate is summarized by Graham (1987); see also Barman (1977, 412). Pang and Seckinger (1972) studied the political elite, not the administrative one. Out of twenty-three prime ministers from 1847 to 1889, as many as fourteen came from Bahia and the Northeast (236). More important, no fewer than eighteen had previous education in law. In 1871–89, out of a total of sixty-three cabinet ministers, fifty-three had received their academic training at one of the two law schools (one in Pernambuco) in the country (Murilo de Carvalho 1982, 385). On the declining political strength of the judicial system during the 1870–80s, see Flory (1975, 1981), especially on the *juizes de distrito*.

3. The decree of 1862 is reproduced in Souto Maior (1978, 21). Strangely enough, Barman (1977) does not even mention it. The variety of measures in Brazil at the time was tremendous. As the Marquess of Olinda pointed out during the debate prior to the decree of 1862: "Existe confusão nos nossos pezos e medidas; a differença não é só de uma província para outra, ha dif-

ferença do systema das capitais das províncias para o interior" (Marcílio and Lisanti 1973, 30). A similar variety existed in Portugal, where a law introducing the metric system was passed in 1852; that is also early.

4. The Emperor had already suggested this measure in 1864 (Burns 1970, 182). As Murilo de Carvalho (1982) points out, the Lei do Ventre livre "was passed over the strong opposition of landowners, who bitterly attacked the government and the Emperor. The approval . . . was made possible by the large number of public employees in the House" (394). Of the latter, most came from the North, now less dependent on slave labor than the coffee economy of the South.

5. Actually, in the Northeast merchants were trying to charge the same price, referring to the new standard units, which were 10 percent smaller than the old ones (Barman 1977, 414f.).

6. On Campina Grande, see Webb (1974, 75). In Areia properties were not very large. There were 1,168 slaves in 1873 (Almeida 1958, 205). Dr. Manoel do N. Machado Portela, who opened an agricultural exposition in Recife on 2 December 1873, emphasized that cotton was almost exclusively grown by free labor. It was easy to explain because it did not require machinery or large buildings or group work. It could be grown by any individual or family. Moreover, as distinct from slaves, such producers would also constitute excellent consumers. But, unfortunately, transports and freights were too expensive. The state had to provide railroads (Mello 1975, 1:27f.). On techniques, see also Stein (1957, 47f.). On labor, see also Eisenberg (1974, 183).

7. Lewin (1987, 50) underscores also that the various *municípios* were often quite heterogeneous ecologically.

8. For total Brazilian cotton exports 1860/61–1875/76, see Stein (1957, 45). On this level, the nadir was not reached until 1875/76. According to the Swedish-Norwegian consul in Pernambuco, F. A. Wegelin, "la récolte des cotons en 1874 démontre de nouveau une déchéance considérable contre celle de l'année précédente." Generally, the economic situation, even worse than in 1873, had now produced "une véritable crise locale." In the course of 1874, Wegelin notes that the exchange rate in London reached a sharp low in May/June—that is, several months prior to the revolts (Swedish National Archives, Stockholm). On cotton prices, see História (1971, 124f.).

9. This movement, called "Ronco de Abelha," was no doubt on a smaller scale than the Quebra Quilos but still comparable. President António Coelho de Sá Albuquerque reported that "estou convencido do que os movimentos populares nesta província não foram o resultado de un plano político anteriormente concebido e meditado e calculadamente executado." Also, an even earlier movement, "a Guerra dos Cabanos" of the 1830s, in the backlands of Pernambuco and Alagoas, may be somewhat comparable to the Quebra Quilos. It was recruited among cotton-producing peasants in the Agreste, too (Andrade 1989, 68–75).

10. To take just one, in Goiana, near Pernambuco's border with Rio Grande do Norte, the Quebra Quilos movement also had an element of xenophobia.

There were some seventy foreigners there, mostly merchants and Portuguese-born (Souto Maior 1978, 119–24).

11. The point is made by a French engineer, Henri Auguste Milet, who had settled down in Pernambuco and published an important account (difficult to locate), "Os quebra-quilos e a crise da lavoura," Recife, 1876, to which both Souto Maior (1978) and S.R.R. de Quiroz (1979) refer. According to Milet, the Quebra Quilos were "grupos numerosos embora *as mais veces desarmados*" (my emphasis) (Quiroz 1979, 31).

12. Even though Almeida (1958) disapproves of the Quebra Quilos rebels, he has to admit that when, in late 1874, 200 armed rebels occupied Areia, "não derramaram sangue nem violaran domicílos" (143). On the other hand, military repression was ferocious (144f.).

13. On 1 March 1875, the Guarda Nacional of the province of Pernambuco counted 944 men. Half of them were stationed in Recife, however. The rest were scattered in small groups in the various towns (Souto Maior 1978, 100).

14. Colonel Da Fonseca takes pain to refuse such accusations. He admits, though, that discipline was not so easy to maintain (Quebra-Kilos 1937, 122–23, 125–27).

15. The Liberals also emphasized the contrast between the misery of the North and the wealth of the South in this connection. Wrote Maciel Pinheiro in the *Diário de Pernambuco* on 11 October 1876: "E o fato é que o Norte morre enquanto o Sul prospera. O levante dos quebra-quilos e o brado de uma população faminta e miserável que ha aínda de fazer-se ouvir mais fortemente" (quoted by Bernardes 1984, 320).

16. On the fall of Rio Branco's government, see, e.g., Calmon (1947, 80). According to Mello (1984), who studied the tax system in the northern provinces thoroughly (247–85), "o movimento dos quebra-quilos viera alertar o Governo imperial para os riscos da desordem fiscal no norte" (261). Still, there was no quick remedy.

17. Della Cava (1968) compares Canudos and Joaseiro; in his book (1970), he only deals with the latter phenomenon. On Canudos, see also Levine (1988). For the *cangaçeiros*, see especially a most readable book by Maria Isaura Pereira de Quiroz (1968).

18. In his report to Rio Branco on 8 March 1875, the Conservative President Lucena of Pernambuco made clear that he did not think that the revolts had an economic background. In late 1874, he had also explained that the tax issue was insignificant, and that the good intentions regarding the recruitment law and the new measures had been misunderstood. The religious question, on the other hand, had been a "mina explorada por aqueles que procuram desvairar os espíritus dos incautos" (Souto Maior 1973, 110–15, quote 112). Almeida (1958, 138) also believes the religious conflict was the real cause of the Quebra Quilos revolts. Thornton (1948, 212–14), on the other hand, argues that the causes were primarily social and economic and that the links with the religious question were merely "tenuous."

19. The Conservative paper, *Diário de Pernambuco*, on 27 November 1874,

reports that the rebels "têm o seu quartel-geral em Alagoa Grande, donde se passarão à cidade de Areia e a esta Capital, conforme o plano por eles assentado" (Joffily 1976, 112). There is no reason to take this rumor seriously, however.

20. According to Barman (1977, 418f.), the spread of the Quebra Quilos movement "was halted partly by the backward condition of the province of Alagoas, whose lack of a developed network of market towns prevented the . . . spread, just as it was to halt the spread of the peasant leagues almost a century later." According to Almeida (1958, 136), the movement spread to nine *municípios* in Paraíba. Of those, seven were located in the Brejos and Agreste zones to the East, where herbaceous cotton was grown. Only two took place in tree-cotton areas of the Sertão (Cabaçeiras, São João do Cariri; see Lewin 1987, 105); the interior of Bahia was also affected (75). Thornton (1948, 212) mentions reactions if not revolts against the new measures also in Pará, Minas Gerais, and Rio Grande do Sul.

21. For the background of the term, see Fourquin (1972, 176–83). In a comment on this chapter, my friend Dr. Matthias Röhrig Assunção of Berlin, a specialist on the rural history of northeast Brazil, on 12 February 1990, rightly observed: "a situação dos labradores pobres . . . variava muito segundo as microregiões. Por isso os conflitos ficaram limitados ao nivel local e não poderam dar origem a um movimento de envergadura regional."

22. To be sure, in the town of Bonito, Pernambuco, according to the *Diário de Pernambuco*, on the 19th of November, a Liberal politician and officer of the Guarda Nacional was one of the leaders of the rebels and was killed in action. "Homens importantes do Partido Liberal insuflavam, abertamente, o povo à sedição" (quoted by Joffily 1976, 113).

23. It should be noted, however, that in Areia, the mob attacked the theater, suspected to be a Mason temple, and destroyed the portrait of the emperor kept there. According to the district judge, "apoderaram-se d'elle e com um frenesi de canibães os esfaquearam e poseram-no em pequenos pedaços no meio de violentas injurias á Pessoa Augusta do Chefe da Nação" (Quebra-Kilos 1937, 117).

24. As Barman (1977) puts it, the Quebra Quilos proceeded with "neatness and economy to reach eminently sensible goals" (417). Possibly relying on him, Burns (1986) also finds the movement to have succeeded in checking the government's new modernizing "drive" (170).

25. On *sujeição*, later on better known as *cambão*, see also Webb (1974, 119f.) and Andrade (1963, 165). For a classical account, see the book *Cambão* by Julião (1972), founder of the Peasant Leagues of the 1950s.

26. On the Guarda Nacional, see also História 1971, 274–98. The reform was decreed on 10 September 1873.

27. In Europe, according to Kula (1980), "the metric system was created by a certain society during a certain stage of its history." Not even in that society (France), however, could it be carried out in isolation. First, the feudal dues had to be abolished, legal equality enforced, and local particularities sup-

pressed. In Europe, "the bayonets of the soldiers of the Revolution did not only carry the meter but also snatched the Crowns from the Royal heads" (432).

28. Graham (1990, 38) considers the Quebra Quilos movement to have been the "most significant protest of the free poor" during the Second Empire (1840–89).

Chapter 6. The Native-born Face the Promotion of Immigration by the State

1. The figure for 1912 is gross immigration. In net terms, 1910, with 208,870 entries, forms the peak because net immigration in 1912 was less, 206,121. In 1911–12, the Italian government banned all emigration to Argentina, due to bad sanitary conditions on immigrant ships (Solberg 1970, 14).

2. For an English version of the 1853 Constitution, see Fitzgibbon (1948, 14–31). It is interesting to compare with the still more generous terms in Alberdi (n.d., 301–3).

3. There were a total of 39,553 naturalizations from 1906 to 1915, with 1911, i.e., the eve of the electoral reform, as the peak year (7,331). The highest numbers were Uruguayans (4.84 percent), Germans, Austrians, and Belgians; the lowest ones were Brazilians and Turks (0.73 percent) (Tercer Censo 1914, 1:212–15).

4. Heaps-Nelson (1978) defines the alternatives and provides an interesting account of the debates preceding the law.

5. Argentine historian Tulio Halperín Donghi (1976) comments: "al hacer del sufragio una base más real del poder político, la democratización agrega sustancia a la división entre nativos e inmigrantes; para un gran partido electoral (= UCR) la tendencia a concentrar sus atenciones sobre los primeros puede ser expresión de un sólido buen sentido antes que de la presencia de prepotentes prejuicios xenófobos."

6. Gallo (1983, 379ff.) provides impressive figures on voter participation in municipal elections in the *colonias* with their foreign-born population in the 1870s.

7. The tax appears to have oscillated between 1.18 and 1.88 percent of the farmers' gross income, 1892–94. On the other hand, from 1893 onward, it contributed around a fourth of the income of the provincial treasury (Gallo 1976, 19ff.).

8. In this connection, it should be noted that in the course of 1893 and 1894, Santa Fé suffered two federal interventions (Gianello 1978, 344).

9. According to Gianello (1978, 370), the year was 1909.

10. Thedy (1909, 90f.). In 1899 already, pressure had been brought to bear upon the provincial assembly to award the immigrants suffrage in all provincial elections. As a compromise, they got it for municipal elections. In 1909, a massive strike against municipal taxation in Rosario, with heavy immigrant participation, enjoyed the League's support (Liebscher 1975, 31, 35, 132–33, 146, 159–62). The tension between "Creoles" and immigrants in southern Santa Fé as late as 1918 has been described by Jefferson (1926), who was there then.

"Creoles, of course, make up almost the totality of political appointees," and some of these public servants "display a good deal of old-fashioned Creole incompetence, sending you to the next window or to some other official" (120).

11. The share of agricultural units not cultivated by the owners in the province rose from 37.6 percent in 1895 to 69.0 in 1914 (Gallo and Cortés Conde 1972, 180).

12. In 1919 there were severe strikes both in North and South. As to the elections of 1920, Lisandro de la Torre (a personal foe of Hipólito Yrigoyen) energetically claimed that they had been fraudulent (Gianello 1978, 379–82).

13. Gallo and Sigal (1965) also elaborated what they call a "modernization index." For this they are criticized by Rock (1975b, 280–85), and we only used the "foreign-born" component here.

14. Between 1870 and 1910, the city grew by a yearly average of 4 percent, a very impressive rate (Scobie 1974, 12).

15. From the point of view of total immigration in Argentina, in 1869 41.8 percent lived in the city of Buenos Aires; in 1895, 34.3 percent; and in 1914, 32.9 percent (Bourdé 1974, 190–93).

16. By 1914, the urban agglomeration had vastly exceeded the boundaries of the federal district in both north and south. Thus, 458,000 *porteños* lived outside the city as such (Bourdé 1974, 112); 41.9 percent of these were foreign-born (Walter 1984, 709).

17. By including only males above nineteen years of age, Germani (1968, 267) gets very high percentages for foreign-born in the city: in 1895, 80 percent; in 1914, 77 percent; in 1947, still 41 percent.

18. Sex ratios (the number of men per 100 women) for Spaniards in the city of Buenos Aires in 1895 were 161 and dropped to 127 in 1914; for Italians, 159 and 160; for native-born, on the other hand, 89 and 93, respectively. Some two-thirds of the immigrants married homogeneously. In 1882–1900, only 16 percent of the total number of births in Buenos Aires were to parents who were both Argentine-born (Baily 1980, 44–46).

19. In 1914, state employees in administration and education in the city of Buenos Aires totaled 50,000—one-twelfth of all employed males but about a fourth of all middle-class males (Rock 1975a, 22).

20. To take a few concrete examples: in 1914, of 6,107 bakers in the city of Buenos Aires, 88.5 percent were foreign-born; of 12,347 shoemakers, 87.4 percent; of masons, 84.9 percent. For the two most numerous groups, servants (88,227) and day laborers (82,506), the percentages were 66.3 and 90.8 (Scobie 1974, 265).

21. As early as 1886–97, the German-language newspaper *Vorwärts* (pro-Socialist) "consistently urged its readers to acquire Argentine citizenship." So also did the pro-Radical *Tagesblatt* (Newton 1977, 26f.). To remain a foreigner, however, had its advantages. Among other things, you were free from military service, which was made obligatory in 1902 (Scobie 1974, 287). Astonishingly, of 764 PS members in 1896, no more than 43 were Argentine citizens. Not until 1915 was citizenship required to enter the party (Baily 1967, 18). In 1911,

social scientist Rodolfo Rivarola published the results of a pioneering poll of almost 2,000 people of various professions. Those foreign-born were probably less than a fifth, though. Socialists totaled 510; 78 percent of them were in favor of extending the vote easily to foreigners, while those of other political views were far more reluctant to do so (Cantón 1968, esp. 96, 103).

22. Under the provisions of the Laws of Residence, according to Socialist *Vanguardia*, by 1916 a total of 383 men had been expelled (Rock 1975b, 82). Not so many, perhaps, but enough to scare!

23. Walter (1978, 597). Because the social distribution of immigrants was so skewed to their disadvantage (not least in the city of Buenos Aires), according to Peter Smith (1974), the 1912 electoral reform implied "that suffrage was effectively extended from the upper class to selected segments of the middle class, to the distinct disadvantage of the lower class, especially the urban working class." Together with the *Lista incompleta* system, it meant that no more than 30 percent of the adult male population enjoyed political representation (11–12). Below, the presentation of election results for the city of Buenos Aires are based on Cantón (1968/69), as presented in Walter (1977).

24. Spalding (1977) asserts that the Socialist "policy of treating working class issues exclusively within a parliamentary context gained little union support. It totally excluded immigrant workers who could not vote. Socialism increasingly appealed to the higher paid members of the working class" (61f.). Rock (1975b, 299f.) gives some examples from the ward (*circuito*) level of how workers came to vote with the Radicals, especially in 1918, 1926, and 1928, on the same high level as citywide.

25. Figures presented in literature vary widely from 65 to 800 Jews killed and from 300 to 4,000 injured (Walter 1977, 155). On the League, see Deutsch (1986a, 1986b). According to Rock (1975a, 79), until 1921, the "League became the country's most powerful political association. It forced Yrigoyen to abandon his hope of winning working class support" and instead promoted repression. The imposition of the state of siege was defended by the radical newspaper *La Época* on 15 January 1919. As distinct from so many previous measures of that kind, it did not threaten civil liberties. Instead it was a defense "ante una invasión extranjera"! Xenophobia had been fomented by several literary writers. Especially influential was José Miró (pseudonym, Julián Martel). In his novel *La Bolsa* (1891, reprinted as late as 1971), as Fishburn (1981, 92f.) puts it, "All immigrants are condemned . . . but one people, the Jews, are singled out as the worst culprits. . . . Within Martel's xenophobia, there is a vein of hysterical anti-semitism."

26. After the failure of Joaquín V. González' proposed labor code 1904 (referred to above) and Yrigoyen's merely temporary and partially successful labor policy, one may, in Latin American terms, agree with Pérez Amuchástegui (1965, 95) that until 1930 Argentine labor "remained free of a state-imposed framework." However, as Korzeniewicz (1989) underlines, even prior to 1907, "there were incipient efforts to introduce state regulation of the labor market and the workplace" (39). On the other hand, obviously, the state also used repression at the behest of employers.

27. The Centro de Almaceneros in 1918 explicitly exhorted its overwhelmingly foreign-born membership to vote in municipal elections, "which are of such great importance to us" (Rock 1975b, 253–54).

28. Walter (1978) has made a sophisticated attempt at analyzing political preferences and social class in Buenos Aires (city) elections, 1912–27. For that purpose he uses no less than eight occupational groups. He finds correlations to be significant. Between Socialist voters and skilled workers they varied from $r = .52$ to $.87$; with semi-skilled and service workers, from $r = .46$ to $.66$. Otherwise, the correlations of Socialist voters to occupational groups were negative. The correlations of Radical voters with "low non-manuals" he finds to have been "positive, ranging from .45 to .71." Published figures on ethnic groups on the circuit (*circunscripción*) level seem to be only available for 1909 (Scobie 1974, 260), but Walter does not discuss this problem. Nor has he seemingly tried to find a breakdown of the election behavior of naturalized citizens, rather numerous from 1912 onward, after all. Our own correlations in the text were based on data in Scobie (1974, 260, 272), Cantón (1968–69), and Walter (1977, 139, 237–38).

29. Also, apparently, the very numerous ethnic mutual aid societies played an important role in the lives of immigrants, as exemplified in an unpublished paper by Rómolo Gandolfo (1988). At the least, they probably defused intra-ethnic conflicts between landlords and tenants or patrons and workers belonging to the same ethnic group.

30. As explained by two geographers, these were the natural conditions: "El calor, alternado con un invierno riguroso, la facilidad y abundancia de riego y la ausencia de humedad atmosférica" (Urien and Colombo 1914, 336). At that time, some 236,000 hectares were under irrigation, thanks mainly to the rivers Tunuyán, Mendoza, and Diamante (342).

31. Native Argentines in Mendoza then totaled 188,583; 82 percent were born in the province. There were only 598 naturalized citizens, 257 of whom were Spaniards and 154, Italians (Tercer Censo 1914, 2:409).

32. Scobie cannot give any figure for 1914 because the manuscript census for that year has been lost. For other heuristical problems, see Fleming (1978).

33. This was the last "election" of the old style. In Mendoza the share of voters rose from only 17 percent in 1910 to 64 percent in 1912, one of the steepest increases in the country (Cantón 1973, 45). The expansion of wine production since 1895 and that of provincial budgets to 1914 are obviously closely related (1,031 and 931 percent); see table 3 and Tercer Censo 1914, 10:353.

34. During Yrigoyen's first presidency, 1916–22, he intervened in Mendoza three times: 24 November 1917 to 6 March 1918, 24 December 1918 to 26 June 1919, and 28 August 1920 to 4 February 1922; under his successor, Marcelo T. Alvear (1922–28), twice: 2 October 1924 to 6 February 1926, and 6 October 1928 to 6 September 1930 (Cantón, Moreno, and Ciria 1972, 90). Yrigoyen was by far the most interventionist president of Argentina so far: he ordered 24 out of a total of 101 interventions between 1860 and 1930 (Gómez 1947, 64, 67).

35. According to Leopold Suárez, provincial Minister of Industries, in 1922, there were then 3,768 *viñateros sin bodegas* with 40,657 hectares of land (56.9 percent) and 1.349 *bodegueros,* who were at the same time *viñateros* with 30,812 hectares (43.1 percent), while 375 *bodegueros* did not own land (Rodríguez 1979, 176).

36. As Jorge Balán sees it, with reference to Mendoza and Tucumán, 1880–1930, "La inhabilitación para ocupar cargos electivos y votar no parecía haberlos inquietado mucho; por el contrario, tenía tantas ventajas como desventajas. En comparación con la oligarquía tradicional cuya vida parecía girar tanto alrededor de la política provincial y nacional, a veces en claro desmedro de su actividad económica, los inmigrantes podían concentrar en ésta todo su esfuerzo" (1978, 79). For the role of wine taxation, see, for example, Balán and López (1977, 423–27).

37. To take San Rafael as a concrete case of political change, in the national elections of 1916, the Conservatives won with 47 percent. In those of 1918, on the other hand, the UCR won with 79 percent of the votes; in the provincial elections of 1922, the Lencinistas won with 69 percent and in 1926 with 59 percent, while the national elections the same year gave them 73 percent in San Rafael. In 1928, however, the UCR recovered the department with 51 percent. In 1930, finally, only six votes distinguished the UCR from the Lencinistas (Cantón 1968, 1:28, 44, 94, 114, 134, 170f.).

Bibliography

Adlercreutz, Federico de. 1928. *La cartera del coronel Conde de Adlercreutz: Documentos inéditos relativos a la historia de Venezuela y de la Gran Colombia*. Ed. by C. Parra-Pérez. Paris: Excelsior.

Alberdi, Juan Bautista. N.d. *Bases y puntos de partida para la organización política de la República Argentina*. Ed. by C. Zavala. 2d ed. Buenos Aires: Estrada. First published in 1852.

Almeida, Horácio de. 1958. *Brejo de Areia: Memórias de um município*. Rio de Janeiro: Ministério da Educação e Cultura.

Alsina, Juan A. 1910. *La inmigración en el primer siglo de la Independencia*. Buenos Aires: F. A. Alsina.

Alvarado, Lisandro. 1956. *Historia de la Revolución Federal en Venezuela*. *Collected Works*, vol. 5. Caracas: Ministerio de Educación.

Anderson, Benedict. 1991. *Imagined Communities: Reflections on the Origin and Spread of Nationalism*. Rev. ed. New York: Verso.

Anderson, Perry. 1979 [1974]. *Lineages of the Absolutist State*. London: Verso.

Andrade, Manoel Correia de. 1963. *A terra e o homem no Nordeste*. São Paulo: Editôra Brasiliense.

———, ed. 1989. *Movimentos populares no Nordeste no período regencial*. Recife: Ed. Massangana.

Annino, Antonio, et al., eds. 1987. *América Latina: Dello stato coloniale allo stato nazione*. 2 vols. Turin: Franco Angelí.

Arias, Abelardo. 1943. *Alamos talados: Novela*. 3d ed. Buenos Aires: Huella.

Armas Chitty, J. A. de. 1961. *Tucupido: Formación de un pueblo del llano*. Caracas: Universidad Central de Venezuela.

Bagu, Sergio. 1969. *Evolución histórica de la estratificación social en la Argentina*. Caracas: Instituto de investigaciones económicas y sociales.

Baily, Samuel L. 1967. *Labor, Nationalism and Politics in Argentina*. New Brunswick, N.J.: Rutgers University Press.

———. 1980. "Marriage Patterns and Immigrant Assimilation in Buenos Aires, 1882–1923." *Hispanic American Historical Review* 60 (1): 32–48.

Balán, Jorge. 1978. "Una cuestión regional en la Argentina: Burguesías provinciales y el mercado nacional en el desarrollo agroexportador." *Desarrollo Económico* 18 (69, Buenos Aires): 49–87.

Balán, Jorge, and Nancy G. Lopez. 1977. "Burguesías y gobiernos provinciales en la Argentina: La política impositiva de Tucumán y de Mendoza entre 1873 y 1914." *Desarrollo Económico* 17 (67, Buenos Aires): 391–435.

Balance. 1989. *Balance de la historiografía sobre Ibero-América, 1945–1988*. Proceedings of the Fourth Conversaciones de Historia. Ed. by V. Vázquez de Prada and I. Olabarri. Pamplona: Editorial Universidad de Navarra.

Banck, G. A., R. Buve, and L. van Vroonhoven, eds. 1981. *State and Region in Latin America: A Workshop*. Amsterdam: CEDLA.

Barman, Roderick J. 1977. "The Brazilian Peasantry Reexamined: The Impact of the Quebra Quilos Revolts, 1874–75." *Hispanic American Historical Review* 57 (3): 401–24.

Benedict, Bradley. 1974. "El estado en México en la época de los Habsburgos." *Historia Mexicana* 23 (4, México): 551–610.

Berdugo y Oquendo, Andrés. 1963. "Informe del visitador real Don Andrés Berdugo y Oquendo sobre el estado social y económico de la población india, blanca y mestiza de las provincias de Tunja y Vélez a mediados del siglo XVIII." *Anuario colombiano de historia social y de la cultura* 1 (1, Bogotá): 131–96.

Bernardes, Denis. 1984. "Notes autour de la pré-industrialisation du Nordeste du Brésil." Pp. 309–21 in Frédéric Mauro, ed., *La pré-industrialisation du Brésil: Essais sur une économie en transition, 1830/50–1930/50*. Paris: CNRS.

Borah, Woodrow. 1983. *Justice by Insurance: The General Indian Court for Colonial Mexico and the Legal Aids of Half-Real*. Berkeley: University of California Press.

Borah, Woodrow, Charles Gibson, and Robert A. Potash. 1963. "Colonial Institutions and Contemporary Latin America." *Hispanic American Historical Review* 43 (3): 371–94.

Bourdé, Guy. 1974. *Urbanisation et immigration en Amérique Latine: Buenos Aires, XIXe et XXe siècles*. Paris: Auber.

Brading, David A. 1974. "Gobierno y élite en el México colonial durante el siglo XVIII." *Historia Mexicana* 23 (4): 611–45.

Brito Figueroa, Federico. 1966. *Historia económica y social de Venezuela: Una estructura para su estudio*. 2 vols. Caracas: Universidad Central de Venezuela.

———. 1973. *El problema tierra y esclavos en la historia de Venezuela*. Caracas: Asamblea legislativa del Estado Aragua.

———. 1975. *Tiempo de Ezequiel Zamora*. 2d ed. Caracas: Centauro.

Bronner, Fred. 1986. "Urban Society in Colonial Spanish America: Research Trends." *Latin American Research Review* 21 (1): 7–72.

Buisson, Inge, et al., eds. 1984. *Problemas de la formación del estado y de la nación en Hispanoamérica*. Bonn: Inter Nations.

Burns, E. Bradford. 1970. *A History of Brazil*. New York: Columbia University Press.

———. 1986. *Latin America: A Concise Interpretive History*. Englewood Cliffs, N.J.: Prentice Hall.

Bushnell, David. 1972. "La evolución del derecho de sufragio en Venezuela." *Boletín histórico* 29 (Fundación John Boulton, Caracas): 189–206.

Calmon, Pedro. 1947. *História do Brasil*. Vol. 4, *O Império, 1800–89*. Rio de Janeiro: Companhia Editora Nacional.

Canak, William L. 1984. "The Peripheral State Debate: State Capitalist and Bureaucratic-Authoritarian Regimes in Latin America." *Latin American Research Review* 19 (1): 3–36.

Cantón, Dario. 1966. *El parlamento argentino en épocas de cambio: 1890, 1916 y 1946*. Buenos Aires: Instituto Torcuato di Tella.

———. 1968/69. *Materiales para el estudio de la sociología política en la Argentina*. 2 vols. Buenos Aires: Instituto Torcuato di Tella.

———. 1973. *Elecciones y partidos políticos en la Argentina: Historia, interpretación y balance, 1910–1966*. Buenos Aires: Siglo XXI.

Cantón, Dario, José Moreno, and Alberto Ciria. 1972. *Argentina: La democracia constitucional y su crisis*. Buenos Aires: Paidós.

Carmagnani, Marcello. 1984. *Estado y sociedad en América Latina, 1850–1930*. Barcelona: Ed. Critica.

Castillo Blomquist, Rafael E. 1987. *José Tadeo Monagas: Auge y consolidación de un caudillo*. Caracas: Monte Avila.

Chevalier, François. 1957. *Significación social de la fundación de la Puebla de los Angeles*. Puebla, México: Centro de estudios históricos.

Cientocincuenta Años. 1963/64. *150 años de vida republicana: 1811–1961*. 2 vols. Caracas: Presidencia de la República.

Codazzi, Agustín. 1841. *Resumen de la geografía de Venezuela*. Paris: H. Fournier.

———. 1960. *Obras escogidas*. 2 vols. Caracas: Ministerio de Educación.

Colmenares, Germán. 1970. *La provincia de Tunja en el Nuevo Reino de Granada: Ensayo de historia social, 1539–1800*. Bogotá: Universidad de los Andes.

———. 1973. *Historia económica y social de Colombia, 1537–1719*. Bogotá: Universidad del Valle.

Concepto. 1966. *El concepto de la historia en Laureano Vallenilla Lanz*. Caracas: Universidad Central de Venezuela.

Constitución. 1959. *La constitución federal de Venezuela de 1811: Estudio preliminar de C. Parra-Pérez*. Caracas: Academia Nacional de la Historia.

Constituciones. 1965. *Las constituciones de Venezuela*. Ed. by Luis Mariñas Otero. Madrid: Cultura Hispánica.

Cornblit, Oscar. 1967. "European Immigrants in Argentine Industry and Politics." Pp. 220–48 in Claudio Veliz, ed., *The Politics of Conformity in Latin America*. London: Oxford University Press.

Crahan, Margaret E. 1974. "Spanish and American Counterpart: Problems and Possibilities in Spanish Colonial Administrative History." Pp. 36–70 in Richard Graham and Peter H. Smith, eds., *New Approaches to Latin American History*. Austin: University of Texas Press.

Dahrendorf, Ralph. 1990. *Betrachtungen über die Revolution in Europa*. Stuttgart: DVA.

Dauxion Lavaysse, J. J. 1967. *Viaje a las islas de Trinidad, Tobago, Margarita y a diversas partes de Venezuela en la América Meridional*. Ed. by Angelina Lemmo and others. Caracas: Universidad Central de Venezuela.

Bibliography

Deler, J. P., and Yves Saint-Geours, eds. 1986. *Estados y naciones en los Andes: Hacia una historia comparativa: Bolivia-Colombia-Ecuador-Perú.* 2 vols. Lima: Instituto de Estudios Peruanos and Instituto Francés de Estudios Andinos.

Della Cava, Ralph. 1968. "Brazilian Messianism and National Institutions: A Reappraisal of Canudos and Joaseiro." *Hispanic American Historical Review* 48 (3): 402–20.

————. 1970. *Miracle at Joaseiro.* New York: Columbia University Press.

Demelas, Marie-Danielle, and Yves Saint-Geours. 1988. *Jerusalén y Babilonia: Religión y política en el Ecuador, 1780–1880.* Quito: CEN.

Depons, Francisco. 1960. *Viaje a la parte oriental de Tierra Firme en la América Meridional.* 2 vols. Caracas: Banco Central de Venezuela.

Deutsch, Sandra McGee. 1986a. *Counterrevolution in Argentina, 1900–1932: The Argentine Patriotic League.* Lincoln: University of Nebraska Press.

————. 1986b. "The Argentine Right and the Jews, 1919–1933." *Journal of Latin American Studies* 18 (London): 113–34.

Díaz Sánchez, Ramón. 1950. *Guzmán: Eclipse de una ambición de poder.* Caracas: Ministerio de Educación Nacional.

Doctrina. 1960. *La doctrina conservadora: Fermín Toro.* Caracas: Sesquicentenario de la Independencia.

Dumond, D. E. 1976. "An Outline of the Demographic History of Tlaxcala." Pp. 13–23 in M. H. Crawford, ed., *The Tlaxcaltecans: Prehistory, Demography, Morphology and Genetics.* Lawrence: University of Kansas Publications in Anthropology.

Dupoy, Walter. 1966. *Sir Robert Ker Porter's Caracas Diary, 1825–1842: A British Diplomat in a Newborn Nation.* Caracas: Instituto O. y M. Blohm.

Eastwick, Edward B. 1959. *Venezuela: Apuntes sobre la vida en una república sudamericana con la historia del empréstito de 1864.* Caracas: Banco Central de Venezuela.

Eisenberg, Peter L. 1974. *The Sugar Industry in Pernambuco: Modernization without Change, 1840–1910.* Berkeley and Los Angeles: University of California Press.

Eisenstadt, S. N. 1963. *The Political Systems of Empires.* Glencoe, Ill.: Free Press.

Eisenstadt, S. N., and L. Roniger. 1984. *Patrons, Clients and Friends: Interpersonal Relations and the Structure of Trust in Society.* Cambridge: Cambridge University Press.

Ensinck, Oscar Luis. 1979. *Historia de la inmigración y la colonización en la Provincia de Santa Fé.* Buenos Aires: Fundación para la educación, la ciencia y la cultura.

Estado. 1974. "El estado político mexicano" (special issue). *Historia Mexicana* 23 (4, El Colegio de México): 93.

Evans, Peter B., Dietrich Rueschemeyer, and Theda Skocpol, eds. 1985. *Bringing the State Back In.* Cambridge: Cambridge University Press.

Fals Borda, Orlando. 1957. *El hombre y la tierra en Boyacá: Bases sociológicas e para una reforma agraria.* Bogotá: Ediciones Documentos colombianos.

Fishburn, Evelyn. 1981. *The Portrayal of Immigration in Nineteenth-Century Ar-*

gentine Fiction, 1845–1902. Berlin: Biblioteca Ibero-Americana, Colloquium Verlag.

Fitzgibbon, Russell H., ed. 1948. *The Constitutions of the Americas, as of January 1, 1948*. Chicago: University of Chicago Press.

Fleming, William J. 1978. "Regional Research in Argentina: A Critical Evaluation of the Archives and Libraries of Mendoza Province." *The Americas* 35: 110–20.

———. 1987. *Regional Development and Transportation in Argentina: Mendoza and the Gran Oeste Argentina Railroad, 1885–1914*. New York: Garland Publishing.

Flory, Thomas. 1975. "Judicial Politics in Nineteenth-Century Brazil." *Hispanic American Historical Review* 55 (4): 664–92.

———. 1981. *Judge and Jury in Imperial Brazil, 1808–1871: Social Control and Political Stability in the New State*. Austin: University of Texas Press.

Forme. 1982. "Forme storiche dello stato" (special issue). *Nova Americana* 5 (Turin: G. Einaudi).

Fourquin, Guy. 1972. *Les soulèvements populaires au Moyen age*. Paris: Presses universitaires de France.

Gallo, Ezequiel. 1976. *Farmers in Revolt: The Revolutions of 1893 in the Province of Santa Fe, Argentina*. London: University of London.

———. 1983. *La pampa gringa: La colonización agrícola en Santa Fé, 1870–1895*. Buenos Aires: Ed. Sudamericana.

Gallo, Ezequiel, and Roberto Cortés Conde. 1972. *Argentina: La república conservadora*. Buenos Aires: Paidós.

Gallo, Ezequiel, and Silvia Sigal. 1965. "La formación de los partidos políticos contemporáneos: La Unión Cívica Radical." In T. S. DiTella et al., eds., *Argentina, sociedad de masas*. Buenos Aires: EUDEBA.

Galloway, J. H. 1971. "Brazil." Pp. 335–99 in Harold Blakemore and Clifford T. Smith, eds., *Latin America: Geographical Perspectives*. London: Methuen.

Galvão, Miguel Arcanjo. 1969. *Relação dos cidadãos que tomaron parte no governo do Brasil no período de março de 1805 a 15 de novembro de 1889*. Rio de Janeiro: Arquivo Nacional.

Gandolfo, Rómolo. 1988. "The Italian Mutual Aid Societies of Buenos Aires: Issues of Class and Ethnicity within an Immigrant Community, 1880–1920." Fifth Latin American Labor Conference, Princeton, N.J. April (draft copy).

———. 1990. "Inmigrantes y política en la Argentina: Notas sobre la revolución cívica de 1890 y la campaña para la naturalización automática de los extranjeros." *Migraciones* 1 (2, Münster): 25–30.

García Müller, Luis. 1986. "Evolución del Hato en Barinas y el comercio del cuero y del ganado." *Tierra Firme* 4 (14, Caracas): 523–36.

García Ponce, Antonio. 1982. *Panorámica de un período crucial en la historia venezolana: Estudio de los años 1840–1847*. Caracas: Academia Nacional de la Historia.

Germani, Gino. 1955. *Estructura social de la Argentina: Analisis estadístico.* Buenos Aires: Ed. Raigal.

———. 1968. *Política y sociedad en una epoca de transición: De la sociedad tradicional a la sociedad de masas.* Buenos Aires: Paidós.

Gianello, Leoncio. 1978. *Historia de Santa Fé.* 3d ed. Buenos Aires: Plus Ultra.

Gibson, Charles. 1952. *Tlaxcala in the Sixteenth Century.* New Haven: Yale University Press.

———. 1966. *Spain in America.* New York: Harper Torchbooks.

Gil Fortoul, José. 1954. *Historia constitucional de Venezuela.* 4th ed. Vols. 2–3. Caracas: Ministerio de Educación.

Gilmore, Robert L. 1964. *Caudillism and Militarism in Venezuela, 1810–1910.* Athens: Ohio University Press.

Gledhill, John. 1988. "Legacies of Empire: Political Centralization and Class Formation in the Hispanic-American World." See Gledhill, Bender, and Trolle Larsen 1988, 302–19.

Gledhill, John, Barbara Bender, and Mogens Trolle Larsen, eds. 1988. *State and Society: The Emergence and Development of Social Hierarchy and Political Centralization.* London: Unwin & Hyman.

Godio, Julio. 1980. *Historia del movimiento obrero latinoamericano.* Vol. 1, *Anarquistas y socialistas, 1850–1918.* México, D.F.: Ed. Nueva imagen.

Gómez, Rosendo A. 1947. "Intervention in Argentina, 1860–1930." *Inter-American Economic Affairs* 1 (3): 55–73.

Góngora, Mario. 1951. *El estado en el derecho indiano: Época de fundación, 1492–1570.* Santiago de Chile: Instituto de investigaciones histórico-culturales.

———. 1975. *Studies in the History of Spanish America.* Cambridge: Cambridge University Press.

González, Margarita. 1970. *El resguardo en el Nuevo Reino de Granada.* Bogotá: Universidad Nacional.

González González, Alfonso F. 1977. *El Oriente venezolano a mediados del siglo XVIII a través de la visita del gobernador Diguja.* Caracas: Academia Nacional de la Historia.

González Guinan, Francisco. 1954. *Historia contemporánea de Venezuela.* Vols. 2–8. Caracas: Presidencia de la República.

González Sánchez, Isabel, ed. 1969. *Haciendas y ranchos de Tlaxcala en 1712.* Introduction, paleography, and notes by Isabel González Sánchez. México: Instituto Nacional de Antropología e Historia.

Gosselman, Carl August. 1962. *Informes sobre los estados sudamericanos en los años de 1837 y 1838.* Ed. by Magnus Mörner. Stockholm: Library and Institute of Latin American Studies.

Graham, Richard. 1987. "State and Society in Brazil, 1822–1930." *Latin American Research Review* 22 (3): 223–36.

———. 1990. *Patronage and Politics in Nineteenth-Century Brazil.* Stanford: Stanford University Press.

Graham, Richard, and Peter H. Smith, eds. 1974. *New Approaches to Latin American History.* Austin: University of Texas Press.

Halperín Donghi, Tulio. 1976. "Para qué la inmigración? Ideología y política inmigratoria y aceleración del proceso modernizador: el caso argentino (1810–1914)." *Jahrbuch für Geschichte von Staat, Wirtschaft und Gesellschaft Lateinamerikas* (Cologne and Vienna) 13:437–89.

Hawkshaw, John. 1975. *Reminiscencias de Sudamérica: Dos años y medio de residencia en Venezuela.* Caracas: Presidencia de la República.

Heaps-Nelson, George. 1977. "Emilio Civit and the Politics of Mendoza." Pp. 4–23 in John F. Bratzel and D. M. Masterson, eds., *The Underside of Latin American History.* East Lansing: Latin American Studies Center, Michigan State University.

———. 1978. "La aprobación de la ley Saenz Peña." *Revista de Historia* 4 (7, Escuela de Historia, Universidad Nacional, Heredia, Costa Rica): 9–26.

Held, David, et al., eds. 1985. *States and Societies.* Oxford: Blackwell.

História. 1971. *História geral da civilização brasileira.* Vol. 2:4, *O Brasil monárquico: Declínio e queda do Império.* São Paulo: Difusão Européia do Livro.

Humboldt, Alexander von. 1970. *Relation historique du voyage aux régions équinoxiales du Nouveau Continent fait en 1799, 1800, 1801, 1802, 1803 et 1804.* Re-edition of 1814–25 original ed. by H. Beck. 3 vols. Stuttgart: Brockhaus.

Iglesia. 1989. *Iglesia, religión y sociedad en la historia latinoamericana, 1492–1945.* 8th Annual Meeting of Asociación Historiadores Latinoamericanistas Europeos (AHILA). 4 vols. Szeged, Hungary: Univ. József Attila.

Izard, Miguel. 1970. *Series estadísticas para la historia de Venezuela.* Mérida: Universidad de los Andes.

———. 1972. "La agricultura venezolana en una época de transición." *Boletín Histórico* 28 (Fundación John Boulton, Caracas): 3–67.

———. 1973. "El café en la economía venezolana del XIX. Estado de la cuestión." *Estudios* 1 (Valencia, Spain): 205–73.

———. 1979a. *El miedo a la revolución: La lucha por la libertad en Venezuela, 1777–1830.* Madrid: Ed. Tecnos.

———. 1979b. "Tanto pelear para terminar conversando. El caudillismo en Venezuela." *Nova Americana* 2 (Torino): 37–82.

———. 1981. "Ni cuatreros ni montoneros, llaneros." *Boletín Americanista* 23 (31, Barcelona): 83–142.

———. 1982. "Oligarcas, temblad, viva la libertad. Los llaneros del Apure y la Guerra Federal." *Boletín Americanista* 24 (32, Barcelona): 227–72.

———. 1987. "Sin fé, sin ley y sin caudillo. Cambio cultural, liberalismo e insurgencias populares." *Siglo XIX: Revista de Historia* 2 (3, Monterrey): 113–31.

Jefferson, Mark. 1926. *Peopling the Argentine Pampa.* New York: American Geographical Society.

Joffily, Geraldo Irenéo. 1976. "O quebra-quilo: A revolta dos matutos contra os doutores 1874." *Revista de História* 54 (São Paulo): 69–145.

Julião, Francisco. 1972. *Cambão, the Yoke: The Hidden Face of Brazil.* Harmondsworth, England: Penguin Books.

Kaplan, Marcos. 1986. "The Theory of the State and the Third World." Pp. 276–92 in Ali Kazancigil, ed., *The State in Global Perspective*. Paris: Gower/UNESCO.

Keane, John, ed. 1988. *Civil Society and the State: New European Perspectives*. New York: Verso.

Kelle, V., and M. Kovalson. 1973. *Historical Materialism: An Outline of Marxist Theory of Society*. Moscow: Progress.

Konetzke, Richard, ed. 1953–62. *Colección de documentos para la historia de la formación social de Hispanoamérica, 1493–1810*. 2 vols. Madrid: Consejo Superior de Investigaciones Científicas.

———. 1983. *Lateinamerika: Entdeckung, Eroberung, Kolonisation*. Gesammelte Aufsätze. Ed. by Günter Kahle and H. Pietschmann. Cologne: Böhlau Verlag.

König, Hans Joachim. 1988. *Auf dem Wege zur Nation: Nationalismus im Prozess der Staats- und Nationbildung Neu Granadas 1750 bis 1856*. Wiesbaden: Steiner.

Korzeniewicz, Roberto P. 1989. "Labor Unrest in Argentina, 1887–1907." *Latin American Research Review* 24 (3): 71–98.

Kula, Witold. 1980. *Las medidas y los hombres*. Madrid: Siglo XXI.

Lacerda de Melo, Mário. 1958. *Paisagens do Nordeste em Pernambuco e Paraíba*. Rio de Janeiro: Conselho Nacional de Geografia.

Lambert, Jacques. 1967. *Latin America: Social Structures and Political Institutions*. Berkeley and Los Angeles: University of California Press.

Landaeta Rosales, Manuel. 1963. *Gran recopilación geográfica, estadística y histórica de Venezuela*. Vol. 1. Colección cuatrocentenaria de Caracas. Caracas: Banco Central de Venezuela.

Langer, Erick D. 1989. *Economic Change and Rural Resistance in Southern Bolivia*. Stanford: Stanford University Press.

Lemert, Charles C., and Garth Gillan. 1982. *Michel Foucault: Social Theory as Transgression*. New York: Columbia University Press.

Levine, Robert M. 1978. *Pernambuco in the Brazilian Federation, 1889–1937*. Stanford: Stanford University Press.

———. 1988. "Mud-hut Jerusalem: Canudos revisited." *Hispanic American Historical Review* 68 (3): 525–62.

Lewin, Linda. 1987. *Politics and Parentela in Paraíba: A Case Study of Family-based Oligarchy in Brazil*. Princeton: Princeton University Press.

Liebscher, Arthur Francis. 1975. "Commercial Expansion and Political Change: Santa Fé Province, 1897–1916." Ph.D. diss. Bloomington: Indiana University.

Lisboa, Miguel Maria. 1954. *Relación de un viaje a Venezuela, Nueva Granada y Ecuador*. Caracas: Presidencia de la República.

Lockhart, James, Frances Berdan, and Arthur J. O. Anderson, eds. 1986. *The Tlaxcalan Actas: A Compendium of the Records of the Cabildo of Tlaxcala, 1545–1627*. Salt Lake City: University of Utah Press.

Lombardi, John V. 1971. *The Decline and Abolition of Negro Slavery in Venezuela, 1820–1854*. Westport, Conn.: Greenwood.

———. 1976. *People and Places in Colonial Venezuela*. Bloomington: Indiana University Press.

———. 1979. "The Rise of Caracas as a Primate City." Pp. 433–72 in David J. Robinson, ed., *Social Fabric and Spatial Structure in Colonial Latin America*, vol. 1. Ann Arbor, Mich.: University Microfilms International.

———. 1985. *Venezuela: La búsqueda del orden, El sueño del progreso*. Barcelona, Spain: Editorial Crítica.

Lombardi, John, Germán Carrera Damas, and Roberta E. Adams. 1977. *Venezuelan History: A Comprehensive Working Bibliography*. Boston: G. K. Hall.

Lynch, John. 1973. *The Spanish American Revolutions, 1808–1826*. New York: W. W. Norton.

———. 1984. "Los caudillos de la Independencia, enemigos y agentes del Estado-Nación." Pp. 197–218 in Buisson, Inge, et al., eds. *Problemas de la formación del estado y de la nación en Hispanoamérica*. Bonn: Inter Nations.

MacLachlan, Colin M. 1988. *Spain's Empire in the New World: The Role of Ideas in Institutional and Social Change*. Berkeley and Los Angeles: University of California Press.

Maeder, Ernesto J. A. 1989. "Las misiones de guaraníes: Historia demográfica y conflictos con la sociedad colonial, 1641–1807." Congresso sobre história da população da América Latina, 2–6 July 1989, Ouro Preto, Seccão 2. Mimeographed.

Malamud, Carlos D. 1991. "Acerca del concepto de 'Estado colonial' en la América hispana." *Revista de Occidente* 116 (Madrid): 114–27.

Mann, Michael, ed. 1983. *The Macmillan Student Encyclopedia of Sociology*. London: Macmillan.

———. 1984. "The Autonomous Power of the State." *Archives européennes de sociologie* 25 (2, Paris): 185–213.

———. 1986. *The Sources of Social Power*. Vol. 1, *A History of Power from the Beginning to* A.D. *1760*. Cambridge: Cambridge University Press.

Maravall, José Antonio. 1972. *Estado moderno y mentalidad social, siglos XV a XVII*. 2 vols. Madrid: Revista de Occidente.

Marcílio, Maria Luiza, and Luis Lisanti. 1973. "Problèmes de l'histoire quantitative du Brésil: Métrologie et démographie." Pp. 29–37 in *L'histoire quantitative du Brésil de 1800 à 1930: Paris, 11–15 Octobre, 1971*. Paris: Conseil National de Recherches Sociales.

Materiales. 1971. *Materiales para el estudio de la cuestión agraria en Venezuela, 1829–1860: Enajenación y arrendamiento de tierras baldías*. Vol. 1., *Estudio preliminar por Carmen Gómez*. Caracas: Universidad Central de Venezuela.

———. 1979. *Materiales para el estudio de la cuestión agraria en Venezuela, 1810–1865*. Vol. 1, *Mano de obra: legislación y administración*. Caracas: Universidad Central de Venezuela.

McFarlane, Anthony. 1984. "Civil Disorders and Popular Protests in Late Colonial New Granada." *Hispanic American Historical Review* 64 (1): 17–54.

McKinley, P. Michael. 1985. *Pre-revolutionary Caracas: Politics, Economy and Society, 1777–1811*. Cambridge: Cambridge University Press.

Bibliography

Matthews, Robert Paul. 1977. *Violencia rural en Venezuela, 1840–1858: Antecedentes socio-económicos de la Guerra Federal.* Caracas: Monte Avila.

Mecham, J. Lloyd. 1966. *Church and State in Latin America: A History of Politico-ecclesiastical Relations.* Rev. ed. Chapel Hill: University of North Carolina Press.

Mello, Evaldo Cabral de. 1984. *O Norte agrário e o Império.* Rio de Janeiro: Nova Fronteira.

Mello, José António Gonsalves de, ed. 1975. *O Diário de Pernambuco e a história social do Nordeste, 1840–1889.* 2 vols. Recife: Diário de Pernambuco.

Memorias. 1973. *Memorias provinciales, 1845: Recopilación y prólogo de Antonio Morellano Moreno.* Caracas: Congreso de la República.

Merkx, Gilbert W. 1973. "Recessions and Rebellions in Argentina, 1870–1970." *Hispanic American Historical Review* 53 (2): 285–95.

Meyer, Lorenzo. 1974. "El estado mexicano contemporáneo." *Historia Mexicana* 23 (4): 722–52.

Meza Lopehandía, Juan N. 1976. "Racionalización del indio en Nueva Granada hacia 1780." *Estudios sobre política indigenista española en América* 2 (Valladolid): 203–24.

Mitchell, Christopher, ed. 1988. *Changing Perspectives in Latin American Studies: Insights from Six Disciplines.* Stanford: Stanford University Press.

Moreno y Escandón, Francisco Antonio. 1985. *Indios y mestizos de la Nueva Granada a finales del siglo XVIII.* Introduction by Jorge Orlando Melo. Ed. by Germán Colmenares and Alonso Valencia. Bogotá: Banco Popular.

Mörner, Magnus. 1961. "The Guaraní Missions and the Segregation Policy of the Spanish Crown." *Archivum Historicum Societatis Iesu* 30 (Rome): 367–86.

———. 1962. "La afortunada gestión de un misionero del Perú en Madrid en 1578." *Anuario de Estudios Americanos* 29 (Seville): 247–75.

———. 1963. "Las comunidades de indígenas y la legislación segregacionista en el Nuevo Reino de Granada." *Anuario colombiano de historia social y de la cultura* 1 (1, Bogotá): 63–88.

———. 1968. *Actividades políticas y económicas de los jesuítas en el Río de la Plata: La era de los Habsburgos.* Buenos Aires: Paidós.

———. 1970. *La corona española y los foráneos en los pueblos de indios en América.* Stockholm: Almqvist & Wiksell and Instituto de Estudios Iberoamericanos.

———. 1983. "Economic Factors and Stratification in Colonial Spanish America with Special Regard to Elites." *Hispanic American Historical Review* 63 (2): 335–69.

———. 1985. *Adventurers and Proletarians: A Story of Migrants in Latin America.* Pittsburgh: University of Pittsburgh Press.

———. 1987. "The Indians as Objects and Actors in Latin American History." Pp. 50–85 in Harald Skar and Frank Salomon, eds., *Natives and Neighbours in South America: Anthropological Essays.* Göteborg, Sweden: Gothenburg Studies in Social Anthropology.

————. 1988. "Immigration into Latin America, Especially Argentina and Chile." Manuscript.

————. 1989. "Immigration in the South Cone of Latin America, 1879–1930: Character and Impact on Different Spatial Levels." Manuscript.

Mörner, Magnus, Julia Fawaz de Vinuela, and John French. 1982. "Comparative Approaches to Latin American History." *Latin American Research Review* 17 (3): 55–89.

Mörner, Magnus, and Charles Gibson. 1962. "Diego Muñoz Camargo and the Segregation Policy of the Spanish Crown." *Hispanic American Historical Review* 42 (4): 558–68.

Mörner, Magnus, and Efraín Trelles. 1985. "Dos ensayos analíticos sobre la rebelión de Túpac Amaru en el Cuzco." Stockholm: Institute of Latin American Studies. Pp. 3–24, mimeographed.

Morón, Guillermo. 1971. *Historia de Venezuela.* Vol. 5, *La Nacionalidad.* Caracas: SRL.

Morse, Richard. 1964. "The Heritage of Latin America." Pp. 123–77 in Louis Hartz, ed., *The Founding of New Societies: Studies in the History of the United States, Latin America, South Africa, Canada and Australia.* New York: Harcourt, Brace and World.

Munck, Ronaldo. 1987. "Cycles of Class Struggle and the Making of the Working Class in Argentina, 1890–1920." *Journal of Latin American Studies* 19 (London): 19–39.

Murilo de Carvalho, José. 1982. "Political Elites and State Building: The Case of Ninteenth-Century Brazil." *Comparative Studies in Society and History* 24: 378–99.

Nava, Julián. 1965. "The Illustrious American: The Development of Nationalism in Venezuela under Antonio Guzmán Blanco." *Hispanic American Historical Review* 45 (4): 527–43.

Navarro, Emilio. 1963. *La revolución federal, 1859 a 1863.* Caracas: Academia Nacional de la Historia José Nuceste Sardí.

Newton, Ronald C. 1977. *German Buenos Aires, 1900–1933: Social Change and Cultural Crisis.* Austin: University of Texas Press.

Nutini, Hugo G. 1976. "An Outline of Tlaxcatecan Culture, History, Ethnology and Demography." Pp. 24–34 in M. H. Crawford, ed., *The Tlaxcatecans: Prehistory, Demography, Morphology and Genetics.* Lawrence: University of Kansas Publications in Anthropology.

O'Donnell, Guillermo. 1978. "Reflections on the Patterns of Change in the Bureaucratic-Authoritarian State." *Latin American Research Review* 13 (1): 3–38.

Páez, José Antonio. 1973. *Autobiografía del General José Antonio Páez.* 2 vols. Caracas: Presidencia de la República.

Palacios, Marco. 1981. "La fragmentación regional de las clases dominantes en Colombia: Una perspectiva histórica." Pp. 41–75 in G. A. Banck, R. Buve, and L. van Vroonhoven, eds., *State and Region in Latin America: A Workshop.* Amsterdam: CEDLA.

Panettieri, José. 1966. *Los trabajadores en tiempos de la inmigración masiva en Argentina, 1870–1910.* Buenos Aires: Universidad Nacional de La Plata.

Pang, Eul-Soo, and Ron L. Seckinger. 1972. "The Mandarins of Imperial Brazil." *Comparative Studies in Society and History* 14: 215–44.

Parra-Pérez, C. 1959–60. *Mariño y las guerras civiles.* 3 vols. Madrid: Cultura Hispánica.

Peck, Donald M. 1977. "Argentinian Politics and the Province of Mendoza, 1880–1916." Ph.D. dissertation. Oxford: St. Anthony's College.

Pérez Amuchástegui, A. J. 1965. *Mentalidades argentinas, 1860–1930.* Buenos Aires: Eudeba.

Pérez Vila, Manuel. 1984. *Perspectivas del siglo XIX venezolano.* Caracas: Universidad Santa Maria.

Phelan, John Leddy. 1967. *The Kingdom of Quito in the Seventeenth Century: Bureaucratic Politics in the Spanish Empire.* Madison: University of Wisconsin Press.

———. 1978. *The People and the King: The Comunero Movement in Colombia, 1781.* Madison: University of Wisconsin Press.

Pierson, Christopher. 1984. "New Theories of State and Civil Society: Recent Developments in Post-Marxist Analysis of the State." *Sociology* 18, 4 (Cardiff): 563–71.

Pietschmann, Horst. 1980a. *Die staatliche Organisation des kolonialen Iberoamerika.* Stuttgart: Klett-Cotta.

———. 1980b. *Staat und staatliche Entwicklung am Beginn der spanischen Kolonisation Amerikas.* Münster, Westfalen: Aschendorff.

———. 1982. "Burocracia y corrupción en Hispanoamérica colonial: Una aproximación tentativa." *Nova Americana* 5 (Turin): 11–37.

———. 1983. "La población de Tlaxcala a fines del siglo XVIII." *Jahrbuch für Geschichte von Staat, Wirtschaft und Gesellschaft Lateinamerikas* 20:223–38.

———. 1987. "Estado colonial y mentalidad social: El ejercicio del poder frente a distintos sistemas de valores. Siglo XVIII." Pp. 427–47 in Antonio Annino et al., eds., *América Latina: Dello stato coloniale allo stato nazione.* 2 vols. Turin. Franco Angelí.

———. 1989. "Les Indes de Castille." Pp. 147–88 in Christian Hermann, coordinator, *Le Premier âge de l'état en Espagne, 1450–1700.* Paris: CNRS.

Pino Iturrieta, Elías. 1987. *Las ideas de los primeros venezolanos.* Caracas: Tropykos.

Platt, Tristan. 1982. *Estado boliviano y ayllu andino: Tierra y tributo en el Norte de Potosí.* Lima: Instituto de Estudios Peruanos.

Poggi, Gianfranco. 1978. *The Development of the Modern State: A Sociological Introduction.* London: Hutchinson.

Política. 1976. *Política y economía en Venezuela, 1810–1976.* Essays of M. Izard, M. Pérez Vila, R. P. Matthews et al. Caracas: Fundación John Boulton.

Poulantzas, Nicos. 1973. *State, Power, Socialism.* London: New Left Books.

Problemas. 1984. *Problemas de la formación del estado y de la nación en Hispanoamérica.* Ed. by Inge Buisson et al. Bonn: Inter Nations.

Quebra-Kilos. 1937. "Quebra-Kilos: Relatório do Comandante das forças imperiaes estacionadas na Província da Parahyba do Norte." *Publicacāo do Archivo Nacional* (Rio de Janeiro) 34:99–164.

Quiroz, Maria Isaura Pereira de. 1968. *Os cangaçeiros: Les bandits d'honneur brésiliens.* Paris: Juilliard.

Quiroz, Suely Robles Reis de. 1979. *Historiografia do Nordeste.* São Paulo: Arquivo de Estado.

Rasmussen, Wayne D. 1947. "Agricultural Colonization and Immigration in Venezuela, 1810–1860." *Agricultural History* 21: 155–62.

Roberts, Bryan R. 1981. "State and Region in Latin America." Pp. 9–39 in G. A. Banck, R. Buve, and L. van Vroonhoven, eds., *State and Region in Latin America: A Workshop.* Amsterdam: CEDLA.

Robinson, David J., ed. 1979. *Social Fabric and Spatial Structure in Colonial Latin America.* Ann Arbor, Mich.: University Microfilms International.

Rock, David, ed. 1975a. *Argentina in the Twentieth Century.* Pittsburgh: University of Pittsburgh Press.

———. 1975b. *Politics in Argentina, 1890–1930: The Rise and Fall of Radicalism.* London: Cambridge University Press.

———. 1986. *Argentina, 1616–1982: From Spanish Colonization to the Falklands War.* London: IB Tauris.

Rodríguez, Adolfo. 1977. *Ezequiel Zamora.* Caracas: Ministerio de Educación.

———. 1981. "Trama y ámbito del comercio de cueros en Venezuela. Un aporte al conocimiento de la ganadería llanera." *Boletín Americanista* 23 (31, Barcelona): 187–218.

Rodríguez, Celso. 1979. *Lencinas y Cantoni: El populismo cuyano en tiempos de Yrigoyen.* Buenos Aires: Ed. de Belgrano.

Romano, Ruggiero. 1987. "Algunas consideraciones alrededor de Nación, Estado (y Libertad) en Europa y América centro-meridional." Vol. 1, pp. 1–21 in Antonio Annino et al., eds. *América Latina: Dello stato coloniale allo stato nazione.* 2 vols. Turin: Franco Angelí.

Rosti, Pal. 1968. *Memorias de un viaje por América.* Caracas: Universidad Central de Venezuela. Original Hungarian ed., 1861.

Salvatore, Ricardo D. 1986. "Labor Control and Discrimination: The Contratista System in Mendoza, Argentina, 1880–1920." *Agricultural History* 60 (3): 52–80.

Santos Martinez, Pedro, ed. 1979. *Historia de Mendoza.* Buenos Aires: Plus Ultra.

Schwartz, Stuart B. 1973. *Sovereignty and Society in Colonial Brazil: The High Court of Bahia and Its Judges, 1609–1751.* Berkeley: University of California Press.

Scobie, James R. 1964. *Revolution on the Pampas: A Social History of Argentine Wheat, 1860–1910.* Austin: University of Texas Press.

———. 1972. "Buenos Aires as a Commercial-Bureaucratic City, 1880–1910: Characteristics of a City's Orientation." *American Historical Review* 77 (4): 1035–73.

———. 1974. *Buenos Aires: Plaza to Suburb, 1870–1910.* New York: Oxford University Press.

———. 1988. *Secondary Cities of Argentina: The Social History of Corrientes, Salta, and Mendoza, 1850–1910.* Completed and edited by S. L. Baily. Palo Alto, Calif.: Stanford University Press.

Skocpol, Theda. 1979. *States and Social Revolutions: A Comparative Analysis of France, Russia and China.* Cambridge: Cambridge University Press.

Smith, Adam. 1887. *An Inquiry into the Nature of the Wealth of Nations,* 6th ed. 2 vols. London: George Bell & Sons.

Smith, Peter H. 1974. *Argentina and the Failure of Democracy: Conflict among Political Elites, 1904–1955.* Madison: University of Wisconsin Press.

Solberg, Carl. 1970. *Immigration and Nationalism: Argentina and Chile, 1890–1914.* Austin: University of Texas Press.

Souto Maior, Armando. 1978. *Quebra Quilos: Lutas sociais no outono de Império.* São Paulo: Nacional.

Spalding, Hobart A., Jr. 1977. *Organized Labor in Latin America: Historical Case Studies of Workers in Dependent Societies.* New York: Harper & Row.

Stein, Stanley. 1957. *The Brazilian Cotton Manufacture: Textile Enterprise in an Underdeveloped Area.* Cambridge, Mass.: Harvard University Press.

Stepan, Alfred. 1978. *The State and Society: Peru in Comparative Perspective.* Princeton: Princeton University Press.

———. 1985. "State Power and the Strength of Civil Society in the Southern Cone of Latin America." Pp. 317–43 in Peter B. Evans, Dietrich Rueschemeyer, and Theda Skocpol, eds., *Bringing the State Back In.* Cambridge: Cambridge University Press.

Stern, Fritz, ed. 1956. *The Varieties of History: From Voltaire to the Present.* New York: Meridian Books.

Supplee, Joan Ellen. 1988. "Provincial Elites and the Economic Transformation of Mendoza, Argentina." Ph.D. diss. Austin: University of Texas.

Szewczyk, David M. 1976. "New Elements in the Society of Tlaxcala, 1519–1618." Pp. 137–53 in Ida Altman and James Lockhart, eds., *Provinces of Early Mexico: Variants of Spanish American Regional Evolution.* Los Angeles: Latin American Center, UCLA.

Szuchman, Mark D. 1980. *Mobility and Integration in Urban Argentina: Cordoba in the Liberal Era.* Austin: University of Texas Press.

Tejera, Miguel. 1986. *Venezuela pintoresca e ilustrada.* 2 vols. Paris: Librería española de D. Schmitz, 1875–77. Facsimile ed. Caracas: Ediciones Centauro.

Tercer Censo. 1914. *Tercer censo nacional levantado el 10 de junio de 1914.* 10 vols. Buenos Aires: Comisión Nacional.

Thedy, Enrique. 1909. "Indole y propósitos de la Liga del Sur." *Revista argentina de Ciencias Políticas* 1: 76–95.

Therborn, Göran. 1980. *What Does the Ruling Class Do When It Rules? State Apparatuses and State Power under Feudalism, Capitalism and Socialism.* London: Verso.

Thornton, Mary Crescentia. 1948. *The Church and Freemasonry in Brazil, 1872–1875: A Study in Regalism.* Washington, D.C.: Catholic University of America Press.

Topic, Steven. 1985. "The State's Contribution to the Development of Brazil's Internal Economy, 1850–1930." *Hispanic American Historical Review* 65 (2): 2–28.

Tosh, John. 1984. *The Pursuit of History: Aims, Methods and New Directions in the Study of Modern History.* New York: Longman.

Tosta, Virgilio. 1987. *Historia de Barinas.* Vol. 2, *1800–1863.* Caracas: Academia Nacional de la Historia.

Tovar Pinzon, Hermes. 1982. "El estado colonial frente al poder local y regional." *Nova Americana* 5 (Turin): 39–77.

Trautmann, Wolfgang. 1981. *Las tranformaciones en el paisaje cultural de Tlaxcala durante la época colonial.* Wiesbaden: F. Steiner Verlag.

Uricoechea, Fernando. 1980. *The Patrimonial Foundations of the Brazilian Bureaucratic State.* Berkeley and Los Angeles: University of California Press.

Urien, Carlos M., and Ezio Colombo. 1914. *Geografía general de la República.* 2d ed. Buenos Aires: Maucci Hnos.

Vallenilla Lanz, Laureano. 1919. *Cesarismo democrático.* Caracas: Estudios sobre las bases sociológicas de la constitución efectiva de Venezuela.

———. 1960. *Disgregación e integración.* [1st ed., 1930.] 2d ed. Madrid: Instituto de Estudios Políticos.

Veliz, Claudio. 1980. *The Centralist Tradition of Latin America.* Princeton, N.J.: Princeton University Press.

Vidales, Carlos. 1983. "Estrategias y tácticas en la rebelión de masas: los comuneros de la Nueva Granada, 1781–82." *Ibero-Americana: Nordic Journal of Latin American Studies* 18 (1, Stockholm): 3–26.

Vila, Marco-Aurelio. 1963. *Aspectos geográficos del Estado Barinas.* Caracas: Corporación Venezolana de Fomento (CVF).

———. 1965. *Aspectos geográficos del Estado Sucre.* Caracas: CVF.

———. 1966. *Aspectos geográficos del Estado Carabobo.* Caracas: CVF.

Villamarín, Juan A., and Judith E. Villamarín. 1979. "Chibcha Settlements under Spanish rule: 1537–1810." Pp. 25–84 in David J. Robinson, ed., *Social Fabric and Spatial Structure in Colonial Latin America.* Ann Arbor, Mich.: University Microfilms International.

Walter, Richard J. 1977. *The Socialist Party of Argentina, 1890–1930.* Austin: University of Texas Press.

———. 1978. "Elections in the City of Buenos Aires during the First Yrigoyen Administration: Social Class and Political Preferences." *Hispanic American Historical Review* 58 (4): 595–624.

———. 1984. "Politics, Parties and Elections in Argentina's Province of Buenos Aires, 1912–1942." *Hispanic American Historical Review* 64 (4): 707–35.

———. 1985. *The Province of Buenos Aires and Argentine Politics, 1912–1943.* Cambridge: Cambridge University Press.

Webb, Kempton E. 1974. *The Changing Face of Northeast Brazil.* New York: Columbia University Press.

Weber, Max. 1978. *Economy and Society: An Outline of Interpretive Sociology.* 2 vols. Ed. by G. Roth and C. Wittich. Berkeley and Los Angeles: University of California Press.

134

Bibliography

Wightman, Ann M. 1990. *Indigenous Migration and Social Change: The Forasteros of Cuzco, 1570–1720.* Durham, N.C.: Duke University Press.

Wright, Winthrop R. 1988. "The Todd Duncan Affair: Acción Democrática and the Myth of Racial Democracy in Venezuela." *The Americas* 44 (4): 421–40.

Zavala, Silvio. 1967. *El mundo americano en la época colonial.* 2 vols. México, D.F.: Porrúa.

Index

Index

Designed by Ed King
Composed by Brevis Press
in Baskerville text and display
Printed by Thomson-Shore, Inc., on
50-lb. Glatfelter Eggshell, B-16, and bound in
Holliston Roxite B